A Fevered Crescent

UNIVERSITY PRESS OF FLORIDA

Florida A&M University, Tallahassee
Florida Atlantic University, Boca Raton
Florida Gulf Coast University, Ft. Myers
Florida International University, Miami
Florida State University, Tallahassee
University of Central Florida, Orlando
University of Florida, Gainesville
University of North Florida, Jacksonville
University of South Florida, Tampa
University of West Florida, Pensacola

A Fevered Crescent

Security and Insecurity in the Greater Near East

☽

James F. Miskel and P. H. Liotta

University Press of Florida
Gainesville/Tallahassee/Tampa/Boca Raton
Pensacola/Orlando/Miami/Jacksonville/Ft. Myers

Photo used in Chapters One and Seven: *Earth Lights*. Data
courtesy Marc Imhoff of NASA GSFC and Christopher Elvidge
of NOAA NGDC. Image by Craig Mayhew and Robert Simmon,
NASA GSFC.

11 10 09 08 07 06   6 5 4 3 2 1

A record of cataloging-in-publication data is available from
the Library of Congress.

ISBN 0-8130-3023-4

The University Press of Florida is the scholarly publishing agency
for the State University System of Florida, comprising Florida
A&M University, Florida Atlantic University, Florida Gulf Coast
University, Florida International University, Florida State University, University of Central Florida, University of Florida, University
of North Florida, University of South Florida, and University of
West Florida.

University Press of Florida
15 Northwest 15th Street
Gainesville, FL 32611-2079
http://www.upf.com

for our children

The human tragedy reaches its climax in the fact that after all the exertions and sacrifices of hundreds of millions of people and of the victories of the Righteous Cause, we have still not found Peace or Security.

—*Winston Churchill*

The true voyage of discovery lies not so much in seeking new landscapes as in having new eyes.

—*Marcel Proust*

Contents

List of Maps and Tables

Maps

Tables

Preface

It is a cliché to say that the world has changed and will continue to change, but change is very much on our minds.

Ironically, while we virtually celebrate change in technology, economic competition, and even basic political structures (such as the nature of the Communist government in China) and bemoan the absence of change in the political structures of the Middle East and in the seemingly ancient tensions between "backward" ethnic and religious groups around the world, we have tended to ignore some underlying changes that will have dramatic and lasting effects on our children and their children.

This book is about these underlying changes and their likely effects on the world at large and in particular on the economically advanced states of North America, Europe, and East Asia. Sections of this work draw upon our earlier work that appeared in the *World Policy Journal, Naval War College Review, Orbis, Parameters, Security Dialogue* and *Mediterranean Quarterly*.

We dedicate this book to our children and their children, and we wish to acknowledge the support that we have received from our families and colleagues.

A New Map

When the cold war ended, scholars, pundits, and policymakers turned to the task of defining the new world order and America's place in it. Some warned of a coming anarchy or the clash of civilizations. Others trumpeted the dawn of an era of peace and prosperity overseen by an empowered United Nations or by a benevolent alliance of the United States and its first world allies. After September 11, 2001, however, dire earlier warnings seemed more prescient than countervailing optimistic assessments had been.

Since that fateful day, when commercial airlines disintegrated on impact with the Twin Towers and the Pentagon, citizens of the United States—and indeed many other countries—have felt only a heightened sense of insecurity. Alongside such insecurity, heightened expectations have arisen that governments—in particular the U.S. government—must increasingly rely on the military as a tool for solving or addressing security issues. Ironically, the greater the reliance on military force to solve problems, the less secure many seem to have become. Why is this so?

We believe that a main reason for this security "disconnect" is that governments have fundamentally misperceived what is happening. It is as though governments have been trying to find their way by means of an antiquated map, only to discover that some of the roads and significant markers no longer exist and that new routes and opportunities for exploration have materialized in previously unknown or unmarked locations. What we need is a new map to read the trends now shaping the world.

One such map is the following "earthlights." It is also available on the National Aeronautics and Space Administration's Web site. The image is a composite of satellite photographs taken over a period of months that recorded the nighttime pattern of lights on the surface of the earth. Obviously, most of the illumination is from city lights, and the result, according to NASA, is a unique measure of "the spatial extent of urbanization."

The light patterns depicted in this map force us to think about some disturbing developments such as the changing size and demographics of cities, particularly in the string of cities that stretches from Lagos, Nigeria, north to Cairo, Egypt, then east and southeast to Karachi, Pakistan, and Jakarta, Indonesia. Less obvious features of the map suggest the increased possibility

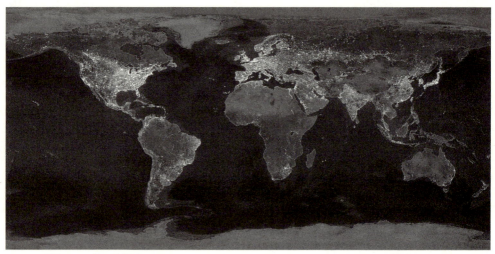

Map 1.1. Earthlights

of failing regions within functioning but troubled states—essentially shad-
owed areas outside the major cities in certain countries, and the rise of ungoverned urban zones in cities that are intimately and inextricably linked to
the rest of the world through the process of globalization. We will examine
each of these trends in some detail, but the broad point can be asserted now:
the effects of these trends will come back to haunt us in the coming decades,
and they are already contributing to our sense of insecurity now.

As one looks at the earthlights image, patterns of world order and disorder begin to emerge, and the patterns do not follow the established boundaries between continents and states. Rather, the patterns suggest that more
basic forces are at play in the globe's physical, economic, cultural, and political geography. For example, the patterns of light stretching east from the Atlantic coastline of Europe into northern Russia clearly suggest that the amal-
gamation of Central and Eastern Europe into an enlarged European Union
may be inevitable, despite the political reservations being expressed today
in some Western European states. Likewise, it seems clear that the fringe of
lights along the North African coastline foretells an inexorable separation of
Morocco, Algeria, and Tunisia from the rest of Africa and the Middle East.
In effect, Muslim North Africa is being drawn like a moth to a bulb into
a European-Mediterranean community, not a Middle Eastern community,
despite cultural and religious ties with the Arab world.

The earthlights image is revealing in other ways as well. India and Pakistan
began their "careers" as independent states at roughly equal political and

economic starting points after the 1947 partition, but since then their paths have been radically and, as the map demonstrates, visibly different. From the altitude of the NASA satellite, all of India appears to be lit. This reflects the industry of its people and the efforts of its public and private sector leaders to become an integral part of the larger world economy through investment in education and infrastructure, the maintenance of domestic stability, and a growing acceptance of global standards and business practices. Conversely, the Pakistan on the map is nearly invisible at night. Pakistan appears dark to the satellite because it has not achieved (or has not been able to achieve) the same level of progress and prosperity that India has apparently secured. One of the reasons why Pakistan may have been unable to build infrastructure and maintain internal stability is that its government has historically had uncertain control over events within its borders. This has effectively discouraged the kinds of domestic and foreign investment that could have lit Pakistan's place on the map.

The same dichotomy is evident on the Korean peninsula, where the 38th parallel forms a stark and disturbing dividing line between North and South Korea. North of the parallel, the area is dark, as it has been for 50 years—testimony to the self-destructive policy of the regime of the Dear and Cherished Leaders—Kim Il-sung and Kim Jong-il. South of the parallel are the bright lights of South Korea, where free enterprise, education, and reasonably good governance have enabled the country to leap from peripheral state to developed nation in a relative few decades.

Dichotomies also exist within states. Canada, Russia, and China are examples. Most of the Canadian lights are within 50 miles of the country's southern border with the U.S. border, and most of eastern Russia's lights hug the track of the Trans-Siberian railroad line. The lights in the People's Republic of China cluster along its Pacific coast, where much of the country's export-led economic growth is based. In none of these countries are the lights as evenly distributed throughout the country as they are in the United States, Taiwan, or Japan. For China, this may suggest the eventual formation of a different set of "two Chinas." Instead of mainland China and Taiwan, there may eventually be a cosmopolitan, densely urban coastal China, including Taiwan, and an underdeveloped and potentially undergoverned interior. There are also two Canadas: a southern Canada in which the majority of the population resides, and an underpopulated north. But Canada is not at risk of the kind of urban overpopulation that plagues cities in Pakistan and other parts of the world. These are not the only examples of dichotomies inside states being caused by the uneven distribution of population. However, when the dichotomies occur in states that are not as well established and capable as these three, security issues may result, as they have in the remote provinces of Pakistan and interior Nigeria.

It is our view that greater attention must be paid to the shadows on the earthlights map—not just North Korea but also the "outbacks" in states being stressed by urbanization such as Pakistan and Nigeria. For a variety of reasons, however, our government and the governments of our allies have tended to focus their foreign and military attention on places where the lights are brightest, even though most of the security threats lie elsewhere. In this sense our policies resemble the approach of the proverbial drunk who drops his keys in the dark and, instead of feeling around for them in the shadows, looks for them under the street lamp because that is the only place where he can see.

The attacks of September 11 did more than convince "Western" populations that they were vulnerable in their own homes. Indeed, the 2004 train bombings in Madrid and the 2005 subway bombings in London reaffirmed the point that at least some threats emanated from enemies whose identity and capabilities were not "in the light." Instead, they came from enemies operating in the shadows. To meet these kinds of challenges of the future, we need to train ourselves to "see" and "think" in the dark.

Traditionally, strategists in Western capitals, not just in Washington, have considered certain types of issues affecting the so-called developing world as deserving less of their attention than arms races, new military technologies, and trade negotiations with other developed states. This approach was manifested in decisions that consigned these issues to often ineffective entities such as the United Nations, nongovernmental organizations, and private sector corporations. The fact that strategists in Western capitals could not be held politically accountable for someone else's failure to solve the developing world's seemingly intractable problems may indeed have contributed to the allure of the "nonstate" prescription. We do not second-guess this prioritization, as these issues were and still are extremely important. However, we believe that there is an emerging understanding that the "nontraditional" security issues that have long plagued the developing world may have started to circle back to haunt us. These issues will be examined in more detail later but deserve introduction here. They include anarchy, governmental collapse, ethnic rivalry inside fracturing states, bitter cultural grievances, religious-ideological extremism, environmental degradation, natural resource depletion, competition for economic resources, drug trafficking, alliances between narco-traffickers and terrorists, the proliferation of "inhumane weapons," cyber war, and the spread of infectious disease. We can try to isolate ourselves from their effects, but as September 11 and the disease warnings about Severe Acute Respiratory Syndrome (SARS) and avian influenza virus (H5N1) make all too clear, perfect isolation is a chimera. As economic globalization proceeds (as it must, international trade and cross-border investment will grow whether or not new free trade agreements are signed), and as the problems and tensions of the dark zones fester, efforts at isolation will be increasingly ineffective.

This is not to say that traditional state-centric security problems are things of the past. Nor is it an implication that military force will necessarily have a substantially smaller role to play in the future. To the contrary, traditional security issues and the tools traditionally used to address them continue to be relevant as the war in Afghanistan, the two Persian Gulf wars, and the aftermath of the second war in Iraq amply demonstrate. Other examples are China's occasionally menacing gestures toward Taiwan and the periodic saber rattling between India and Pakistan. North Korea's acquisition of nuclear weapons and Iran's apparent desire to follow suit indicate very clearly that both states face and pose traditional military threats. All of these examples demonstrate the inescapable point that maintaining certain levels of traditional military capability must remain a central consideration for governments.

Our concern, however, is that while the military in the United States has been wrestling with the challenge of developing ever more impressive means of deterring and defeating "in the light" threats, no agency of government at the state or multi-state level (such as the United Nations and its instrumentalities, or regional structures such as the European Union, NATO, the African Union, the League of Arab States) is doing enough to understand and overcome the threats that are taking shape in the shadowy and dark areas on the earthlights map.

Thus the real question is not whether to concentrate on traditional, "hard" security issues, which normally derive from the friction that arises in the relationships between states, or on "soft" nontraditional security issues, which are not confined by national boundaries. It would be a mistake to pick either of these choices. The right answer is to choose both, and the challenges are first how to widen the aperture on our figurative cameras so that we can see in the dark as well as in the light and to devise a balanced approach to both areas. This book represents our attempt to explain why this wider focus on the "new" map is crucial and to suggest ways it can be translated into effective action.

As our understanding of security concerns broadens and deepens, traditional assumptions about the state and government agencies being the sole guarantors of security will—and should—be increasingly challenged. This is because security may depend on how well we cope with the broader human dilemma that is taking shape around the world. Addressing this dilemma will require sustainable development strategies and must take into account such critical factors as: population growth, particularly in the emerging world; the rapid spread of epidemic diseases; climate change, including shifts in precipitation patterns and rising sea levels; scarcity of potable water; soil erosion and desertification; and increased urbanization and the growth of "megacities" around the globe.

We maintain that particular attention must be paid to urbanization in the Lagos-Cairo-Karachi-Jakarta arc. The populations of these particular cities and many other cities in some parts of Africa and Asia are predicted to surge due to high birth rates and migration from the countryside. Many of these cities lack the infrastructure to support rapid, concentrated population growth, and as a result cities could, in the not so distant future, become platforms for the export of instability, disease, and severe pollution—not to mention home to evermore grinding deprivation and domestic violence. As we will discuss in greater detail in subsequent chapters, the very effort that weak national governments will be compelled to expend in managing the problems of their too-fast-growing cities will most likely result in inattention to other important issues with security consequences for the rest of the world.

To emphasize one particular issue, for example, most of the states in the Middle East are already experiencing water scarcity. Jordan, Kuwait, Saudi Arabia, Israel, and Yemen have been classified as suffering from water scarcity since 1990, and some states have per capita water availability rates that are significantly lower than the minimums recommended by the World Health Organization. As the population of these countries grows and continues to urbanize, water can only become increasingly scarce. Water scarcity will also play a critical role in the Arab-Israeli dispute.

The differences between Israel's low natural population growth rate and the high rates in the West Bank and Gaza Strip as well as in neighboring Arab states mean that Israel will be demographically swamped unless it aggressively promotes immigration—the very thing that water scarcity and terrorism seem likely to discourage. Past surges in immigration to Israel have occasioned outbursts of terrorist violence by Palestinians who understood that as the Israeli population grew, their prospects for recovering historic Palestine diminished. Even if a surge in immigration to Israel were to occur, it could very well spark conflict between Israel, the Palestinian Authority, and neighboring Arab states as it would signal both a stronger Israeli state and increased consumption of the region's water and other natural resources

Table 1.1 Percentage of world urban population

	1950	1975	2000	2030
More developed regions	60	48	32	21
Less developed regions	40	52	68	79

Source: *World Urbanization Prospects*, 2003 revision, data tables and highlights (New York: United Nations Department of International Economic and Social Affairs, 2004), 4.

by Israel. Indeed, the demographic trends suggest that however the Israeli-Palestinian confrontation is resolved—if it ever is resolved—the real power struggle in the region will eventually revolve around natural resources.

The Megacity

Truly cataclysmic demographic changes are taking shape in the Lagos-Cairo-Karachi-Jakarta arc, which we call a "fevered crescent." According to the National Intelligence Council's *Global Trends 2015: A Dialogue about the Future with Nongovernment Experts*, as well as data compiled by the National Geographic Society and the United Nations Population Division, world population will reach 7.2 billion in 2015, up from 6.1 billion in 2000. Ninety-five percent of the growth will take place in "emerging" countries, and nearly all projected population growth will occur in urban areas.

It may be a surprising fact to Westerners used to thinking about New York or perhaps Tokyo as the archetype of the contemporary city that urbanization is actually more a characteristic of the less developed world than it is of economically advanced regions. In fact, according to the United Nations' *World Urbanization Prospects* report, about 40 percent of the world's urban population was in less developed regions in 1950, but by 2030, the percentage is projected to more than double to 80 percent. That is to say, in 25 years, 8 out of 10 of the world's city dwellers will reside in cities that are in relatively poor or desperately poor countries.

In 1950, four of the world's largest cities in terms of population were New York, London, Paris, and Moscow. In 2015 the five largest cities will be Tokyo, Mumbai (Bombay), Lagos, Dhaka, and Sao Paulo. Only Tokyo is certain to be able to manage the challenges of urbanization effectively. Lagos and Dhaka seem doomed to fail.

Of course, the challenge of urbanization is not confined to these five cities. In 2015, there will be 59 cities with populations of 5 million or more and another 23 with populations of at least 10 million. All but a handful of these megacities will be in less developed regions, and it is from these regions that many of the nontraditional security threats of the future will emerge.

A brief look at individual cities will illustrate the enormity of the challenge that the municipal and national governments in some states will face in managing urban growth.

The population of the greater New York metropolitan area, which stood at 12 million in 1950, is projected to grow to 17.6 million by 2015, an increase of "only" 30 percent over a span of 65 years. Moreover, the pace of growth in the city's population will have slowed to 6 percent over the last 15 years. By way of comparison, the population of Nigeria's capital city of Lagos is expected to have grown from 1 million in 1950 to more than 24 million in 2015. Lagos already had a higher population density than New York in 2000 and its population will have doubled again between 2001 and 2015.

Another instructive comparison to help gauge the extent of the challenge that urbanization will present to some states is between Los Angeles and Karachi. While the population of Los Angeles is projected to have increased from 4 million in 1950 to 14.2 million in 2015 (a 350 percent increase over 65 years), most of the growth has already taken place. Indeed, its population will, like New York's, be relatively stable in the early twenty-first century. Conversely, Karachi's population will explode from 1.1 million in 1950 to 20.6 million in 2015. Unlike Los Angeles, almost a third of Karachi's dramatic growth will take place between 2001 and 2015.

Urbanization in and of itself is neither good nor bad. Tokyo's population is projected to reach 28.7 million in 2015, for example, but Tokyo will certainly be far better equipped to handle the infrastructure requirements of the megapopulation than will most cities of the emerging world. Seventy-two percent of Japanese already live in cities, and Japan has accommodated itself to an urbanized existence. However, many of the megacities in the Lagos-Jakarta crescent will be unable to expand their infrastructure and public services quickly enough to keep pace with projected population growth rates. Indeed, few cities in North America and Europe would be able to accommodate 50 or 60 percent increases in population over a period of only 15 years.

Dhaka, the capital of Bangladesh, is an extreme example of a city that will be stressed by growth. In 1950 its population was only 400,000. In 2015 its population is projected to be almost 50 times greater. If the projections hold true, Dhaka will have 19 million residents in 2015. If the population of the greater New York metropolitan area had grown at a similar rate since 1950, in 2015 it would have had a population of 600 million, roughly twice the current population of the United States. If New York's growth rate had matched Dhaka's for only the 2001–2015 time frame, the Big Apple would

Table 1.2 Population in 2015

	Cities with 5 million	Cities with 10 million
More developed regions	11	4
Less developed regions	48	23

Source: World Urbanization Prospects, 2003 revision, data tables and highlights (New York: United Nations Department of International Economic and Social Affairs, 2004), 4.

have a population of 33 million. As it seems unlikely that even a city in the world's richest country could handle such rapid growth, it is difficult to conceive how an impoverished state such as Bangladesh could accommodate such a dramatic population surge in its capital city. The same point can be made for many of the burgeoning cities in Africa, South Asia, and Southeast Asia.

By 2015 there may be more than 600 cities worldwide with populations in excess of 1 million inhabitants. By contrast, in 1950 there were only 86 such cities. As Richard J. Norton noted in the August 2003 issue of the *Naval War College Review*, many of the megacities of the future may well become virtual Petri dishes of instability, disease, and terrorism. In other words, at least some of these cities will grow far beyond the "natural" carrying capacity of their respective national governments, with the result that governmental infrastructure and public services will be stretched past the breaking point.

Further compounding the problem posed by rapid urban population growth is the "youth bulge" phenomenon. In the near future, almost half of the adult populations of many African, Middle Eastern, and Southwest Asian countries will be between the ages of 15 and 29. Despite the recent spate of Chechen and Arab suicide bombings by women, young men are responsible for most acts of criminal and terrorist violence. As the overall population grows, so too will the population of young males looking for employment and educational services, and the cities of the developing world are not well positioned to satisfy the demand for education and job opportunities. Urban disorder, crime, and perhaps extremist political violence may result if these conditions continue, as seems likely, for extended periods.

Cities in this condition will pose a particularly serious security threat to their states and to the world because they will not only have substantial pockets of darkness within their municipal boundaries, but also extensive commercial, communications, and transportation links. In other words, it will be easy for groups in these urban pockets of darkness to export instability.

Pockets of Darkness

The issue of state failure began to be widely discussed in the 1990s. Instead of the peace dividend that appeared to have been promised at the end of the cold war, instability and a collapse of governance at the state level appeared to be on the rise as Somalia, Haiti, and Liberia grabbed the headlines. These and other "failed states" were seen by many as breeding grounds for anarchy and violence and as natural homes for terrorists, warlords, ethnic militias, holy warriors, criminal gangs, arms dealers, and drug merchants. Policy makers hoped that research into state failure might provide early warning indicators that would trigger timely international interventions to prevent collapse. To this end the Central Intelligence Agency established the State Failure Task Force to conduct a comprehensive examination of the issue. Yet, as events of the past few years have illustrated, there are other bubbling Petri dishes that deserve greater attention—pockets of darkness in under-governed areas within functional but struggling states.

The parastates that take shape in these pockets of darkness (for example, the warlord-dominated "tribal areas" of Afghanistan and the militia-run enclaves in Bosnia and Kosovo) develop what we consider *Night of the Living Dead* characteristics. Possessing some of the functional aspects of statehood, but lacking the civic equivalent of balanced, flexible limbs, these figurative zombies stagger into the future, unable to function independently without massive and continuous life support—in the form of UN aid, or bilateral assistance from other states, or "export earnings" from various criminal enterprises. These parastates or lawless zones inside functioning states present greater threats to international stability than do failed states. Examples include eastern Colombia where narco-terrorists have operated for years inside remote valleys; the "lawless" triangle where Brazil, Paraguay, and Argentina meet and where Hizbullah, arms dealers, and smugglers of all stripes conduct business freely; the hinterlands of the Democratic Republic of Congo, where opposing rebel groups, invading armies, and gangs pillage the countryside and terrorize the people; and Afghanistan beyond the outskirts of Kabul and Kandahar. Due to the stress of managing urban growth, many states will be forced to reduce their presence outside their "Kabuls" and "Kandahars," perhaps creating governance vacuums in which new lawless zones can emerge.

Other pockets of darkness are likely to form around semi-urbanized collections of displaced populations. Tens of millions of refugees, for example, now live in semipermanent camps in the West Bank and Gaza, Sudan, and the Great Lakes region of Africa. These camps, veritable slums with their swollen populations, have in some cases evolved into virtual parastates and are fertile grounds for instability. Palestinian refugee camps, for example, have provided bases of operation for terrorist groups, and (until they were disestablished in 1996) Rwandan refugee camps in the eastern provinces of the Democratic Republic of Congo were the staging grounds for attacks into Rwanda and for intervention in the DRC civil war. The only saving grace from a security viewpoint is that the displaced are typically not well connected by road, rail, or air to the rest of the world and thus may be less efficient exporters of violence to distant locations.

Finding a Way Out

In a world that is becoming more interconnected economically and physically, it is impossible to separate zones of light from pockets of darkness. Many of the states that will be most adversely affected by demographic pressures and rapid urbanization are already entwined in the globalization process and are simply too important to be left to their own devices. Each for somewhat different reasons perhaps, Nigeria, Egypt, Pakistan, and Indonesia very clearly fall squarely into this category. They are struggling—not failed—states whose stability, or lack thereof, will influence security and economic trends throughout the world.

We must encourage internal public sector reform and public security improvements in states such as these where governments are currently failing to keep the lights lit, or where urban population growth is likely to lead to failure at the municipal level or compel overstretched national governments to ignore developments in remote, underpopulated rural areas. One of the undeniable lessons of September 11 is that our security and the security of people throughout the developed world is affected by domestic governance shortcomings elsewhere. Unfortunately, the United Nations, by virtue of its own inefficiency, the divergent agendas of its leading members, and its orientation toward state-level solutions, is not up to the task of promoting effective public sector reform. A more flexible approach is called for. The efforts of all of the actors in the international community need to be better organized, but this organization is not possible without first acknowledging why better organization is necessary. Governments, international organizations, international nongovernmental organizations, national civil society organizations, and for-profit corporations all need to recognize the challenges that urbanization in the developing world will present.

As Jonathan Lash, president of World Resources Institute, has aptly put it, what we need is a "shift from the stiff formal waltz of traditional diplomacy to the jazzier dance" of issue-based networks and creative partnerships. Future strategies must move beyond policing actions and military interventions toward active prevention of resource scarcity and governance failures. Active prevention was the central premise of the strategy of cooperative security, developed by former secretary of defense William Perry and others at the Brookings Institution shortly after the end of the cold war. The idea was to prevent discontent from leading to internal armed conflict by creating jobs, reducing poverty, and improving governance—especially in urban areas—before aggrieved groups resorted to violence. Strategies of preemptive war and forced regime change followed by nation building in essence call for the military to "kick in the door" and then "put the door back on." There are plainly situations where the door does need to be kicked in and a new one popped back on the hinges, but it seems clear that such strategies are ill-suited for many challenges that lie ahead.

A few heretics (most notably Robert D. Kaplan, the author of *The Coming Anarchy*) claim that development—not poverty—leads to unrest by raising expectations. The destabilizing effects of rising expectations are undeniable, but in this wired and interconnected world, expectations are likely to continue to rise no matter what national governments do with regard to economic development. The destabilizing effects will be most dramatic in struggling states with overpopulated cities.

Unfortunately, the typical response to situations of such complexity is to do nothing. That cannot be the response of the United States or of other developed countries. The first order of business must be to promote a sense of urgency. Approaches must be devised for radically improving public infrastructure and governance in the states where high levels of urban growth are projected. The cities and states in what we call the fevered crescent deserve particular priority because of their size, regional influence, strategic location, and economic connections. Because many are Islamic, there is an ideological reason as well—events in these cities and states could well exacerbate tensions with the West.

Unless actions are started soon to contain, if not reverse, the worrisome trends outlined here, we are likely to be in for decades of military engagement and increased insecurity. Rather than justifying intervention, we ought to be thinking about investment. When we look at the map of the lit and unlit world, we can see where work needs to be done.

Pockets of Darkness

The emerging geography and environment depicted in the previous chapter focus on two major features of the map of the future: overcrowded, under-governed cities and underpopulated, undergoverned rural areas in countries across an arc from Lagos to Cairo, to Karachi and Jakarta. Both features of this landscape are of concern but for somewhat different reasons.

Fast-growing and overgrowing cities create serious environmental and security problems. They may also serve as virtual breeding grounds for disease, domestic instability, and terrorism. In some countries, urban growth will put particularly stressful demands upon governments. Indeed, many of the countries in which these growing cities are located already have governments that have been struggling to meet the demands of their citizens for economic opportunity and law and order. It is virtually inevitable that some national governments will respond to the challenge of managing rapid urbanization by prioritizing their energies in ways that effectively reduce the amount that is invested in the governance of areas remote from the major urban areas. This is likely to result in the formation of what we have called pockets of darkness—zones where the government is either unable or unwilling to maintain control and that appear as shadows on our earthlights map because they are home to little or no modern economic activity. These pockets are not, of course, actually depopulated; they may instead be populated by small villages that support themselves by traditional forms of agriculture and perhaps increasingly by criminal and terrorist organizations.

Terrorism, of course, ranks among today's top security challenges, and the trends highlighted in this book strongly suggest that it will continue to be a challenge for decades. In this chapter we examine in more detail the phenomenon of undergovernance in remote districts and its potential relationship to the threat of terrorism in the coming decades.

Even as the world's overall population grows, the size of the world's rural population will decline slightly or stabilize at current levels over the next 30 years.[1] Given the increased productivity of modern farming technology, this trend will not affect the ability of the world to feed itself and may represent a natural and beneficial economic progression—just as the economy of the United States grew as the proportion of workers engaged in agriculture decreased. By 2030, more than 60 percent of the world's population will be urban and almost all of the growth in urban populations will be in less developed regions. The urban populations of Europe and North America are expected to increase only slightly between 2000 and 2030.

The result is that in 2030 the total urban population of Africa will be 80 percent as great as the combined urban populations of North America and Europe. In 2000, the equivalent percentage was 38 percent.[2] As urban populations grow, the political power of the countryside must diminish, and this will reduce the incentive for national governments to invest scarce governance resources (gendarmeries, effective courts, infrastructure maintenance personnel and equipment) anywhere but in the collective city. In Nigeria, for example, the urban population will grow from 44 percent of the total population in 2000 to 68 percent in 2030.

As national governments struggle to manage the consequences of rapid urban growth by trimming their investment in remote, rural areas, the result may be that there will be more opportunities for the emergence of "para-states" and dark zones—territory occupied by small groups with no pretensions of statehood and no desire for anything other than to be ignored by national authorities. In some respects, one may think of the "agency" areas in northwest Pakistan as the models for this phenomenon.

There is an understandable tendency to attribute the virtual independence of Pakistan's tribal agencies—the mountainous badlands along the northern border with Afghanistan—to the ferocity of the tribes in physically rebuffing incursions and their stubborn insistence upon adhering to old ways. This is, however, less than half the story. As formidable as the tribes may have been since the days when the British raj implanted itself on the subcontinent, the reality is that the survival of tribal autonomy depends very heavily upon the fact that the land is without substantial economic resources and has, until very recently, been of virtually no strategic value to anyone other than the affected tribes. That is to say, given the paucity of resources in the region, neither the British East India Company in the eighteenth century, the British government in the nineteenth, nor the Pakistan government in the twentieth regarded the benefits of gaining control over the agencies to be worth the effort of first wresting power from provincial warlords and then maintaining effective governmental structures there. For somewhat the same general reason—the absence of a strong incentive to actually govern remote or not easily accessible rural areas inside a country—new models of tribal "agency areas" are likely to emerge even as the Pakistani versions persist as a result of population pressures in the cities and the challenges of municipal governance.

Terrorist organizations will use these dark zones as bases of operation and as safe havens. This will enable them to take advantage of the "host" nation's sovereignty as a protective shield against action by international law enforcement agencies or foreign militaries. Admittedly, the integrity of the sovereignty shield has been weakening in recent years, but for parastates and terrorist organizations, some such protection is certainly better than none, and as we have seen in both Pakistan's agency areas and the outback of Afghanistan, there is also protection in the very remoteness of the safe haven. While it is certainly possible that al-Qaeda will eventually be suppressed by international law enforcement efforts and American military initiatives, other terrorists or major criminal operations will take their place.

The opportunities for terrorist groups to use these pockets of darkness as bases of operations do not, of course, cause terrorism. Opportunity is passive and does not compel individuals or groups to take maximum advantage of the situations presented. The poverty and isolation of rural pockets of darkness do not present an opportunity in the traditional sense of the word; moreover, the terms themselves are relative. Note, for example, the difference between dollar denominated measures of income and "purchasing power" measures, which better indicate what an individual can acquire in his or her local economy, and neither takes fully into account the social and family supports that mitigate the sting of poverty in traditional societies. Further in the era of globalization, modern communications and transportation networks ensure that no area can be absolutely isolated. Even relatively isolated locations can connect with the larger world, and as we have noted, the connection enables influence to flow both in and out of the pocket of darkness. What concerns us is this ability of the organizations inside the pockets of darkness to project influence outward.

In other words, even in combination with rural isolation, poverty does not necessarily make an individual become a terrorist, just as resource scarcity does not compel groups to attack other groups. Profiles of al-Qaeda members compiled by a former CIA analyst, for example, demonstrate that many members of terrorist groups were from reasonably well-off families, and most September 11 suicide-hijackers were from upper-middle-class Saudi families.[3]

Obviously, the individuals who donate money that ends up in the coffers of terrorist organizations are not themselves poor, although it is conceivable that their donations may have been at least partly motivated by concern about the poverty of the population that the terrorist organization purports to represent. At least some of the donations, for example, the tens of thousands of dollars that are given to the families of Palestinian suicide bombers, do significantly improve the economic conditions of the individual perpetrator's immediate survivors. On the other hand, if poverty were the primary concern, the donor presumably would have contributed directly to poor families, as is indeed the tradition of the *zakat* in some Muslim countries, or to charitable organizations with no affiliation to terrorist groups.

That said, however, conditions of impoverishment do create incentives that apparently do cause individuals to take actions they otherwise might not. These incentives can generate recruitment opportunities for terrorist groups. It is true that an opportunity observed in retrospect by analysts may not have been as obvious to the individuals who could potentially have acted upon them. However, the incentives presented by conditions in the festering urban neighborhoods that burst the seams of municipal and even national governance will be blatantly obvious to groups looking to build a following for dramatic action.

The characteristics of the rural pockets of darkness that should concern us are visible today in eastern Colombia, interior Central Africa, the Iguazu triangle at the confluence of the Brazil-Argentina-Paraguay borders, and in Afghanistan before the war (and perhaps, regrettably, in the Afghanistan that emerges after NATO and American forces withdraw). All except Colombia are relatively poor in terms of industry, traditional agriculture, and indigenous natural resources. Governmental inattention has allowed each to evolve into a nutrient-rich Petri dish for criminal and terrorist organizations.

Colombia

For many years, Colombia has been torn by violence and terrorism. During the 1940s, it endured a civil war between ruling factions known as "la Violencia." But since then the pattern of violence has shifted toward revolutionary uprising, counterrevolutionary response, and conflict among drug-trafficking factions and between the factions and the government. The Revolutionary Armed Forces of Colombia and the National Liberation Army have been fighting against the government and right-wing paramilitary groups for more than four decades. Both so thoroughly control some regions of the country that the United Nations reported in 2003 that in those regions they "have replaced the Government in important aspects of public life, including the use of armed force."[4]

One effect of the violence has been to accelerate migration from the countryside to the cities, particularly the capital, Bogota. According to estimates by Amnesty International, 2 million people have fled from the countryside in recent years in order to avoid violence.[5] Since 1985 some 300,000 Colombian citizens have been killed in both urban and rural settings, and many targets of violence have been among the elite elements in society—four presidential candidates, 200 judges and investigators, half the Supreme Court's justices, and over 150 journalists.[6] Much of this violence qualifies as terrorism. Judges and their families have been assassinated in order to create fear inside the government and to reduce public confidence in the government. Newspaper reporters have been killed to silence them and to frighten their colleagues and editors into softening their coverage of the paramilitaries. Public and private sector infrastructures have been bombed in order to demonstrate the ineffectiveness of the government and to make the affected populations dissatisfied enough with the status quo to withdraw support from the government or to relocate to other areas. Finally, peasants have been killed and their farmsteads burned down to frighten others into abandoning their villages. Judging by the fact that 2 million people have indeed been "displaced" into cities, the violence has achieved its goal of clearing much of the land of uncooperative campesinos. To briefly revisit the argument made earlier in this chapter about poverty not being a cause of terrorism, in this case the poor are the most frequent targets of the violence. Although there are still political aspects to the violence, the prize is the drug trade—an enterprise that has traditionally flourished in valleys and hillsides outside the effective reach of the law enforcement and military arms of the government.

Among the most unusual features of the situation in Colombia is the size of the pocket of darkness where the government's writ does not run. As recently as 2002, about 30 percent of the country was in effect administered by the paramilitaries. Another unusual feature is the amount of money generated by the drug industry in the areas outside government control. Colombia is the world's largest producer of cocaine and is also a major producer of heroin. For our analysis, however, the most significant feature is the length of time that the pocket has remained dark. Eastern Colombia has been virtually autonomous since the 1970s, and the autonomy became more than virtual in 1998 when the government of Andres Pastrana ceased military action in the region as part of an effort to negotiate an end to the fighting. The cease-fire in the region ended in 2002. Since then, the government has made limited progress in eastern Colombia despite substantial aid from the United States under Plan Colombia.[7]

The fact that some territories have been outside government control for nearly 40 years is important because it means that nongovernment groups (in this case, criminal and terrorist organizations) have had enough time to embed themselves in virtually all aspects of the territories' economic and political life. This will make the eventual assertion of government control extremely arduous and will require persistent effort over many years. Efforts to assert government control could, moreover, be resisted by terrorist actions, and the terrorism could be internationalized in order to reduce foreign support for the Colombian government.

Although they have not had the long-distance reach associated with the September 11 attacks on the United States, it is certainly conceivable that this will not always be the case. The ubiquity of low-cost transportation, itself a feature of globalization, has made it easy for small groups to assemble in distant lands for terrorist purposes, and the drug trade generates more than enough money to fund major international terrorist operations.

Events in Colombia already have had direct transnational effects in South America. Brazil, Venezuela, Panama, and Ecuador have each been adversely affected. These four states have suffered an influx of refugees, cross-border kidnappings, and occasional cross-border incursions by armed Colombian groups. Obviously cross-border incursions are a serious infringement of the national sovereignty of the affected state. These effects are in addition to drug and weapon smuggling.[8] These events clearly threaten to destabilize the larger Andean region. The Panamanian and Ecuadorian governments are not politically strong in the first place, and all of the affected states already face serious economic challenges that can only be exacerbated by influxes of refugees and violence along their borders with Colombia.

Central Africa

The Great Lakes region of Africa has been the scene of violence and anarchy for decades, the most disturbing example of which was the genocide in Rwanda, which will be discussed more in a subsequent chapter. The 1994 genocide was both preceded and followed by civil wars, first in Rwanda and then in the Democratic Republic of Congo.

One of the consequences of the Rwandan civil war that followed the 1994 genocide was the exodus of hundreds of thousands of refugees from Rwanda into eastern Zaire (now the Democratic Republic of Congo, which will subsequently be referred to as DRC). The refugees included a significant number of fighters from the losing side in the Rwandan civil war who used the refugee camps in DRC as a base of operations for attacks into Rwanda. Factions among the Rwandan refugees quickly became engaged in DRC politics by cooperating with local separatist groups, and eastern DRC has been wracked with violence ever since.[9] In 1994 there was a successful rebellion against the central government in Kinshasa (this rebellion led to the renaming of the country), and afterward, a series of mutinies and new antigovernment uprisings, and a more or less continuous series of local-ized ethnic conflicts. There have also been invasions by the militaries of the neighboring countries of Rwanda and Uganda and intervention in defense of the DRC government by Zimbabwe, Namibia, Angola, and Chad. Sudan has supported three guerrilla movements that use eastern DRC as a base of operations against Uganda.[10] Finally, there have been three peacekeeping interventions: two by the United Nations and one by the European Union under a UN charter.[11]

The UN peacekeeping force in DRC (MONUC) is still in DRC and was the subject of considerable controversy in 2004 and 2005. MONUC members have been accused of sexually abusing local women and, more important from the perspective of this book, for "standing idly by" while civilians were attacked. Despite the MONUC's reputation for passivity, nine members were killed in an ambush in December 2004, the sixth year of the mission.[12]

There has been a considerable amount of terrorism in the DRC pocket of darkness, but most of it has remained "local." That is to say, the overwhelm-ing majority of victims have been the families who live in the area or in nearby border villages in Burundi, Rwanda, and Tanzania. Civilian officials associated with the DRC government and the governments of neighboring states have also been targeted. The "only" international targets of terrorism have been humanitarian relief workers and UN officials who came into the pocket.

What is important to note about this particular pocket of darkness is that the anarchy in the region was well known to the outer world and that it has continued due to the inability of the DRC government to assert control over the region and occasionally even over its own armed forces. The reluctance of the United Nations and the international community at large to take de-cisive action to suppress the fighting and establish and maintain order was, of course, also a factor. The EU peacekeeping mission, Operation Artemis, was empowered and equipped to take decisive action against the fighting, but its mandate was geographically narrow (essentially a single province in eastern DRC) and lasted only from June through September 2003.

Whether the functions of establishing and maintaining order in a remote location with wide-scale violence is within the competence or jurisdiction of the United Nations or any other international body can, of course, be debated. Our view is that there is no international organization that would be up to these tasks, and in most similar situations there are no individual nations that have both the capability of and the interest in establishing and maintaining order. This is one of the things that concerns us most about the map of the future: the international community may be as reluctant as it has been in DRC to take decisive action in the pockets of darkness that will take shape in the future.

One thing is quite clear. The international community cannot plead ignorance in explaining its tepid action in eastern DRC. Agencies of the United Nations ran some of the refugee camps from which Rwandan factions operated and clearly understood the destabilizing effects they were having in DRC. UN agencies have continued to provide humanitarian services in the region and have routinely submitted situation reports about the ongoing violence to their headquarters. That these reports had an influence at the highest levels of the United Nations seems to be demonstrated by numerous Security Council Resolutions expressing concern about the violence and calling for the parties to settle their disputes without more violence. There were, for example, four UN Security Council Resolutions on the situation in DRC in 1999, five in 2000, three in 2001, and three in 2002.[13] In 2003 there was even evidence in some UN agency reports of cannibalism in the region.[14] The violence in the regions was also highlighted by the international media and by numerous nongovernmental organizations such as Christian Aid, Médecins Sans Frontières, and Human Rights Watch.

The fighting has been fueled by more than the ethnic resentments of minority groups and provincial dissatisfaction with the ways in which the DRC central government attempts to rule and allocate government resources. Although there is no significant industry in eastern DRC, there are enough easily exploited raw material resources in the region to inspire local groups to fight each other. Indeed, the various factions in eastern DRC have been pillaging the resources in order to buy weapons and recompense their members. The key resources in the region are diamonds, lumber, and coltan, which is used to manufacture cell phones.[15] These natural resources have the same deleterious effects as Colombia's drugs: they provide ready sources for funding of violent groups.

Iguazu

The Iguazu triangle has long been an infamous smugglers' entrepôt. In 1998, for example, the *Wall Street Journal* reported that one "entrepreneur" smuggled three plane-loads of personal computers into Brazil each week.[16] Located at the intersection of the Parana River and the east-west Pan American Highway and two north-south highways, the three points of the triangle are Puerto Iguazu (Argentina), Ciudad del Este (Paraguay), and Foz do Iguaçu (Brazil), but the centroid of the illicit activity is Ciudad de Este. Despite its unsavory reputation, Ciudad del Este has the second largest population of any city in Paraguay. With a population of 200,000, Ciudad del Este is not, strictly speaking, rural, nor is it without modern industries. The city hosts more than 50 banks, which testifies more to the volume of money laundering and the sheltering of illicit gains than to the value of the city's legitimate commerce or the financial acumen of its citizens.

Ciudad del Este is the hub of a rural area that is remote from the urban centers of Brazil and Argentina, and the border controls in the area for all three states have traditionally been lax. In the case of Paraguay, this laxity may have been deliberate. Under the Stroessner regime (1954–1989), elements of the government actively connived at smuggling, and the country has long been known as being indifferent toward the regulation of goods transiting its territory.

In 2004, there were 20,000 Middle Eastern Muslims living in the triangle, and most worked in Ciudad del Este. There have been reports that various Islamist groups have been establishing contacts and raising funds in the triangle.[17] The State Department's *Patterns of Global Terrorism* report for 2000 indicated that the triangle was the "focal point" of Islamist activism in South America.[18] The 2003 *Patterns* report indicated that Hizbullah and Hamas were actively raising funds among the Muslims in the area.[19] Many of the Muslims in Ciudad del Este are of Lebanese extraction and may rationalize their contributions to Hizbullah on the basis of Hizbullah's participation as a political party in Lebanon's elections. A Library of Congress study in 2002 listed the following Islamist organizations as being active in the triangle raising funds, recruiting members, and plotting terrorist attacks elsewhere: al-Qaeda, Hamas, Hizbullah, Egypt's Al-Gama'a al-Islamiyya (Islamic Group), and Al-Jihad (Islamic Jihad). The Library of Congress report also indicated that the planning for terrorist attacks included the recruitment of "sleeper cells," small groups who would move to other parts of the world and blend in with the local population awaiting instructions for a terrorist operation, similar to the September 11 hijackers, who had lived in the United States for months before receiving orders from al-Qaeda.[20]

Our concern here is not to prove that the triangle is a hub of Islamic radicalism, or that Islamist activity in the triangle poses a clear and present danger to the West. It is rather to point out that diaspora populations are attractive sources for fund-raising, especially perhaps when they are engaged in illegal or "gray market" behavior with high profit margins in geographic locations that are of limited strategic or economic interest to the great powers and where there are virtually no effective financial regulations or border controls by the parent national government(s).

Even before the September 11 terrorist attacks, Brazil, Argentina, and Chile had been concerned about the consequences of Islamist activism in and around Ciudad del Este. Argentina experienced a terrorist attack against a Jewish community center in Buenos Aires in 1994, and Hizbullah is suspected of having been involved in it.[21] In 1998, Brazil, Argentina, and Chile began to discuss ways to monitor terrorist fund-raising by Islamists among the Muslim population in the triangle.[22] Since then, the United States and the three triangle states have joined in a "three plus one counterterrorism dialogue" to improve financial controls and border management in the region, and the triangle states have made progress in arresting suspected terrorists.[23]

Afghanistan

According to news reports from Pakistan in November 2004, the former leader of the Taliban government in Afghanistan vowed to "retake control" of that country.[24] In the unlikely event that this were to occur and the status quo ante were restored, the entire country of Afghanistan might revert to what it was in the late 1990s, a huge pocket of darkness. In effect, Afghanistan before the 2001 war (and, if Mullah Omar succeeds, perhaps again in the future) represents a Texas-sized equivalent of the Iguazu Triangle with the important exception that international terrorists were obviously more active in Afghanistan than they have proven to be in Iguazu.

Afghanistan under the Taliban has sometimes been categorized as a "failing" or "failed" state, meaning a state whose government is unable to perform the essential functions of government: collecting taxes, ensuring that a modicum of public services are provided, and asserting the right of sovereignty by defending the state's territorial integrity. Between the period of the Soviet withdrawal from Afghanistan in 1989 and the Taliban accession to power in 1996, Afghanistan was consumed by civil war and may have merited the appellation of a failed state. But after the Taliban won the civil war, that was no longer the case. Under the Taliban, the government successfully prosecuted ongoing combat against its rival, the Northern Alliance, and gradually increased its control over the national territory to 90 percent in 1999. The government also collected taxes on opium poppy crop values and provided services to the citizenry.[25] There were two levies on opium (and other crops): peasants with naturally watered fields paid a 10 percent tax, whereas peasants whose fields were irrigated paid only 5 percent. A third of the revenues from these taxes was used for aid to poor people; the rest went into the government's general budget. The traditional *zakat* tax—

the Islamic religious levy that is to be used to help the indigent—was also charged against opium crops, and the Taliban taxed heroin laboratories and export shipments.[26] In addition, the Taliban provided a number of services that would be considered inappropriate in many parts of the world (enforced restrictions on educational curricula and school attendance, the attire of individual citizens, and social practices as diverse as the interactions between men and women and listening to music). These are very clearly signs of something other than the inability to deliver public services.

Any government that can enforce such regulations, collect taxes, redistribute income to poor villages, and successfully fight off a rebellion is demonstrably competent to perform many of the essential functions of government. The competence may have been misguided by nonfundamentalist lights, but it is nevertheless competence.

One of the ways in which the Taliban government maintained its hold on power was by securing the support of the al-Qaeda terrorist organization. In short order, the Taliban government was benefiting from al-Qaeda's financial and military support, and al-Qaeda members became key advisers to the government.[27] Many believe that it was al-Qaeda's influence that led the Taliban government to destroy the historic Buddhist statues at Bamiyan, which provoked a worldwide outcry.[28] This interpretation was confirmed in private conversations by one of the authors with individuals who have been part of the post-Taliban government in Afghanistan since 2002.

In return, al-Qaeda obtained free and protected access to territory that was used for training and indoctrination facilities, depots for weapons and other logistics support, and an organized setting in which its allies, Islamist extremists from all of the continents, could be housed while undergoing training and planning terrorist operations. Al-Qaeda also received protection from the government, which resisted American and United Nations pressure to bring Osama bin Laden to trial for his involvement in pre–September 11, 2001, attacks on American embassies in Kenya and Tanzania and on a Navy ship in Yemeni waters.[29]

Implications of These Cases

Each of these brief case reviews tells us something important about the pockets of darkness phenomenon. Colombia's struggle with guerrillas and *narco-traficantes* demonstrates both the potential durability of a pocket, even in the face of sometimes erratic and belated governmental and international opposition and the possibility that events in the pocket will destabilize not just the parent country but also neighboring countries. Even discounting the extremely negative effects of drug abuse in the Andean region, it is clear that the violence in Colombia is having spillover effects on Ecuador, Panama, Venezuela, and Brazil.

Spillover effects on other countries were also evidenced in the eastern DRC, where the results have included a continental war and recurrent military incursions by neighboring countries to put a stop to cross-border raids. As recently as December 2004—10 years after the Rwandan refugees surged over the border and began using refugee camps as bases for operations back inside Rwanda—the government of Rwanda was so concerned about the continuing cross-border raids from DRC that it threatened another intervention.[30] The DRC case also demonstrates that under certain conditions, such as extreme violence among local factions that can (and in DRC actually did) spill over onto United Nations peacekeepers and humanitarian aid workers, the international community is unlikely to take decisive action to establish order in a pocket of darkness. The DRC also stands as a warning of the difficulty that intelligence agencies of outside powers will experience in attempting to understand the political, cultural, and military dynamics inside the pocket of darkness, and this may (and probably should) reinforce their reluctance to attempt to establish order there.

According to the U.S. Central Intelligence Agency's *World Factbook 2002*, there are 200 ethnic groups in DRC, and it is frankly unrealistic to expect either the international community as a whole or a select group of major powers to invest in developing the intelligence programs that would be necessary for potential interveners to understand ahead of time the dynamics of the relationships among these ethnic groups, as well as the microeconomic incentives, political grievances, and cultural beliefs that motivate them. This is an unfortunate but inevitable consequence of the fact that some (perhaps most) pockets of darkness develop in areas in which the major powers have no important economic or security interests. This may be changing as a result of the war on terror, but based on its course so far, the war on terror appears to change the priority accorded to "low interest" states only after a terrorist connection has been identified, rather than beforehand as part of a preventive strategy.

The role that refugees and refugee camps played in the decade of anarchic violence in eastern DRC also reminds us that pockets of darkness may form around semipermanent collections of "displaced" populations. There are, for example, tens of millions of refugees who have been forced to live in what amount to favelas or shantytowns in another country. The Rwandan camps in DRC may be an extreme example in the sense that they housed a large number of fighters with both the desire and ability to continue participating in the fight back in Rwanda and with ethnic ties to local minority groups in DRC with their own set of grievances over conditions in the region. The latter, of course, gave the refugees figurative license to meddle in DRC politics.

More established refugee camps, such as the 50-year-old Palestinian camps in the West Bank, have effectively become permanent structures and have been virtually incorporated into the Palestinian municipalities that have grown around them. (In a sense it is peculiar to consider the West Bank and Gaza camps as refugee camps at all because they are physically in "Palestine.") Such camps present a different set of problems—urban problems, really—than do the isolated camps that sprinkle the borderlands of many countries. The Palestinian camps often stumble despite international support, fail to provide the opportunities and services that their occupants demand, and create fertile ground for instability.

The lesson of the Iguazu case is that criminal activity is something that terrorists have learned to take advantage of, at least in terms of fund-raising. This was apparently also the case in Sierra Leone, where there have been allegations that al-Qaeda has been involved in diamond smuggling.[31] Fund-raising for illicit activities is always the most effective where the potential donors have access to large amounts of money or marketable commodities and operate in an environment of lax law enforcement. This aptly describes conditions in the Iguazu triangle, the areas of Colombia and Afghanistan controlled by drug lords, and the eastern provinces of the DRC. Iguazu also reminds us that under certain circumstances nations have acted and presumably will continue to act to establish order in a pocket of darkness. On the other hand, Iguazu may be unusual in that there has been little violence in the triangle (at least in comparison with the fighting in DRC and Colombia), and under these circumstances Argentina and Brazil are clearly capable of improving financial and border controls without incurring the scope of costs that Pakistan would in asserting itself over its agency areas.

Afghanistan demonstrates the importance that local cultures and power dynamics have and, like DRC, how little interest intelligence agencies in North America, Europe, and now East Asia have had in such "local" topics in distant places with little strategic or economic value, at least as measured by traditional metrics—the volume of trade, the presence of vital commodities like oil, military prowess, strategic location astride an important canal or strait. The Clinton administration, for example, was criticized for not taking developments in the Afghanistan pocket of darkness seriously enough.[32] Indeed, decisive action was not taken by the United States until after the September 11, 2001, attacks by a terrorist organization that was based in

Afghanistan and, even then, openly after the Afghan government refused to take action on its own to bring the organization to justice. The timing of the U.S. action was ultimately a reflection of an administration-spanning judgment that Afghanistan was simply not, in and of itself, economically or strategically important to the United States. It was not the result of timidity or myopia in the Clinton White House.

It may be the case that the al-Qaeda organization understood the low priority that events in Afghanistan were accorded in Washington and the capitals of Western Europe and assumed, correctly, that the low priority would give it freedom to continue to operate base camps and prepare to conduct terrorist operations. This further demonstrates a fact that experience has presumably made clear to violent and criminal organizations in other pockets of darkness—that being "off the radar" of the West is tactically beneficial.

Three—and perhaps all four—pockets of darkness that we have briefly examined have been platforms for international terrorism. (The jury is still out on Iguazu, as allegations about sleeper cells being recruited there have yet to be proven.) Only Afghanistan, however, has been a platform for launching terrorist operations against the United States or another major Western power. The reasons obviously have much to do with ideology, as only al-Qaeda has sought to directly challenge the United States outside its home region. The violence in DRC and Colombia have been principally directed against regional and local targets, occasionally including in-country agents of the United States or other Western countries.

Another reason is that the anarchic chaos of DRC and Colombia may make them less desirable as hosts for bases and other terrorist infrastructure, though obviously not for fund-raising. Terrorist organizations must also be concerned that without mastering the complex relationships among ethnic groups, tribes, families, and criminal organizations in places such as eastern DRC, they will run the risk that one or more of these groups will turn on them in order to gain a tactical advantage against another group or for financial or political gain. In other words, some of the factors that discourage preventive measures by the United Nations and its leading members on behalf of government efforts to exert control over remote anarchic provinces may also discourage terrorist organizations with truly international ambitions from building extensive bases of operations there.

All of the case studies reflect, in different ways, the crucial difference that government incompetence or incapacity makes in allowing (or in the case of Afghanistan under the Taliban, choosing to enable) pockets of darkness to form within their borders. As we have noted, it is likely that many national governments (especially in the Lagos-Cairo-Karachi-Jakarta crescent) will be so stressed by managing the challenges of dramatic urban growth that new and potentially destabilizing pockets of darkness will be allowed to form in the future. It is highly likely that many of these pockets of darkness will form in regions of low economic and strategic value to the West.

Geography and Technology Make a Difference

Although pockets of darkness can develop in many terrains (lowlands along a river as in the Iguazu triangle, rugged mountain ranges as in the northwest territories of Pakistan and Afghanistan north of Kandahar, lush tropical valleys in Colombia, and the rolling hills and high grasses of eastern DRC), some terrains offer particular benefits to terrorist organizations. A tactical goal of all terrorist groups is, of course, to prevent intervening military forces from achieving complete success at restoring stability and government agencies from subsequently maintaining order. With respect to this tactical goal, it is clear that terrorists have experienced considerable success in places like Somalia, Iraq, and Afghanistan. They have been able to achieve this success by effectively and creatively taking advantage of the physical landscape. To some extent, new technologies may enable traditional military forces to overcome some of this advantage, but it remains to be seen if this will translate into lasting success at maintaining order in pockets of darkness.

There are distinct differences between terrorists and traditional security forces, and these differences help explain why some terrorists have been adept at taking advantage of their surroundings. Arthur Waldron of the University of Pennsylvania, for example, has described war in the ideal type as having three distinct phases: engagement, chaos, and chopping off heads (*jiaofeng, luan, zhan*). The master of this "intellectual" approach to warfare, of course, is Sun Tzu, who employs *jiaofeng, luan,* and *zhan* through instantaneous, differential shockwave application. Yet when traditional (especially American) security forces speak of "cutting off and killing" an enemy, they mean "to chop heads" in the metaphorical sense; when the terrorist speaks of *zhan* or its linguistic equivalent in a different culture, he is being literal—indeed, Islamist terrorists in Iraq during 2004 have actually videotaped and proudly invited television stations to broadcast the taped decapitations.

That said, new operational concepts and force employment did produce an advantage in crushing the Taliban and al-Qaeda forces in 2001. Another key factor was the existence of motivated indigenous forces, principally the Taliban's long-standing and still-standing rivals in the Northern Alliance. This led to battlefield success, though not necessarily to strategic victory.

Moreover, the Taliban and al-Qaeda made a classic mistake in Afghanistan: they attempted to fight back. They failed to understand that geography and the environment were suddenly less advantageous due to American co-option of Northern Alliance forces that were equally well adapted to the geography and new tactics for dealing with the landscape of Afghanistan. These new tactics included forward positioned special forces units who blended into the environment and could physically relocate in a functional way by calling in precise air strikes instead of attacking the targets on the ground.

It seems worth recalling that five decades ago, Roger Trinquier claimed in *Modern Warfare: A French View of Counterinsurgency* that contemporary war is an interlocking system of political, economic, psychological, and military actions and conflicts. Trinquier argued that armies tend to fight traditional forms of warfare, but that in modern counterinsurgency war they are doomed to failure despite overwhelming firepower. American military success in Afghanistan suggests that with the advent of network warfare and remarkable advances in military technology, Trinquier's gloomy prophecy may not be as set in stone as some once believed when engaging with terrorists using environment and geography to their advantage. However, even as the United States has the capacity to bring massive firepower onto the battlefield—along with an increasingly sophisticated network of intelligence systems, information architecture, unmanned systems, and joint and combined force operations—we should expect to see terrorists increasingly employ environment and geography to advantage in future engagement.

Increased battlefield awareness, the likely increased future use of special operations forces and indigenous forces, precision major fires delivered by various means, and rapid maneuvers to cause the enemy to break, as well as what one observer has called the phenomenon of "marines turned soldiers," has fundamentally altered how wars are fought, at least by the United States.

History has shown that in every single military engagement since the end of the cold war developments such as these have enabled the United States to dispatch its adversaries with relative ease on battlefields and in direct engagements. This would seem to be an argument against continuing investment in ongoing transformation of the armed forces. Why bother, after all, to change the military when no one else can stand up to it? As logical as this argument may sound, true transformation involves human at least as much as technological change. As Larry K. Smith phrases it:

> Overwhelming force implies, almost by definition, a lack of precision. That won't work now. What we're going to need is a much greater

emphasis on the concentrated application of street smarts. I call these sorts of operations "closework." They are extremely precise missions that are used when the results are absolutely crucial. They demand the very highest standards of intelligence, of training, of preparation, of timing and execution. We haven't been particularly good at this in the past.[33]

"Closework" suggests engagements such as the building-by-building/street-by-street operation in closed-off neighborhoods of Fallujah, Iraq, in late 2004 and the hillside-by-hillside engagements of small units that continue in Afghanistan. If these represent, as seems likely, at least one of the faces of twenty-first-century combat, then traditional security forces may need to rely on more than warfare fought at a distance and precision weapons engagements that are not actually precise enough. The process of research and development into the hardware and equipment optimized for the "closework" of counterterror and counterinsurgency operations must continue at a brisk pace because one cannot assume that the terrorists of tomorrow will make the same mistakes that the Taliban forces made in 2001 during Operation Enduring Freedom.

Equally, there are technological means that can help us look through the figurative darkness in ways never thought possible, to find trends and indicators that suggest terrorist activity, especially in remote regions. Specifically, as noted in the 9/11 Commission report, the use of remote sensing in rural areas can provide tremendous advantages. Douglas S. Way, a professor at Ohio State University and chief scientist at Earth Satellite Corporation, has argued that terrorist organizations are adopting some of the "basing" strategies that were employed by guerrilla leaders in the past (Mao, Castro, and Guevara). Each of these leaders used remote, relatively inaccessible areas as bases of operation early in their insurgencies. Mao's 1,000-mile march, for example, took him and his followers away from the capital and coastal cities, into the rugged interior where government troops would have a hard time locating his forces and mounting operations against them.[34] Way and others thus developed global open-source GIS datasets at one-kilometer resolution and maps that show the potential advantages of environment and geography for terrorist groups—in effect where rural pockets of darkness are likely to be used by terrorists in the future. The areas that have been identified are not particularly surprising. Very broadly speaking, they include the northern branches of the Andean mountains and the Amazonian jungle—particularly in the far west (from Rio de Janeiro) and the north where the jungle edges into southern Venezuela and Guyana and Surinam, the interior of Central

Africa, the mountainous regions across Afghanistan and Pakistan, the dense jungles of Southeast Asia, and the rugged islands in the Indonesian and Philippine archipelago. None of these areas have traditionally been accorded high priority in terms of intelligence gathering and monitoring, although that may be changing due to the war on terror and, in some areas, due to the needs of global economy for natural resources.

Indonesia has already witnessed the efficacy of the strategy of basing insurgencies in hard-to-access districts. Not only did Indonesia lose one of those districts (East Timor) but it has been unable to completely suppress similar separatist movements at both its eastern and western tips. Insurgent movements in Aceh province in the east and Irian Jaya in the west have benefited from their distance from Jakarta. Similarly, insurgent movements in the southern Philippines have managed to resist Manila for decades. Indonesia's travails with separatist movements, in fact, point out one of the ironies of international relations in the era of globalization. The restive provinces are far enough away from Jakarta to make military action by the central government arduous. But they are close enough to the international media and to other states to ensure that Indonesia's military and police operations are widely criticized when they are perceived as being too heavy-handed or when the separatist spokesmen are more media-savvy than the government representatives. This, in turn, creates pressure on Indonesia to do less, not more, in terms of asserting its control over the restive provinces. Similarly, the government of Colombia has been strongly criticized for committing human rights abuses in its efforts to suppress insurgents.

This is not to say that the governments do not deserve criticism. They do, but our intent is only to point out that in a curious way, insurgencies benefit from being simultaneously far from the central government and close to international organizations and international media. Terrorist organizations, particularly ideologically driven groups with real or potential sympathizers in other countries, obviously understand the value of this "far-close" proposition. If the al-Qaeda leadership is, as is widely suspected, located in the outback of the Afghanistan-Pakistan border, it is far enough from Kabul and Islamabad and close enough to Al Jazeera and other media outlets.

Cities of Hope, Cities of Fear

Neighborhoods in a city that have a considerable amount of crime, decaying infrastructure, and inadequate public services are not peculiar to the twenty-first century or to municipalities in the developing—or, more appropriately, the majority—world. The novels of Charles Dickens reflect similar conditions in nineteenth-century London, then the leading city in what was arguably the world's most economically advanced country. In *Bleak House* Dickens described one London thoroughfare as a

> black, dilapidated street, avoided by all decent people; where the crazy houses were seized upon, when their decay was far advanced, by some bold vagrants, who, after establishing their own possession, took to letting them out in lodgings. Now, these tumbling tenements contain, by night, a swarm of misery. As on the ruined human wretch, vermin parasites appear, so these ruined shelters have bred a crowd of foul existence that crawls in and out of gaps in walls and boards; and coils itself to sleep, in maggot numbers, where the rain drips in; and comes and goes, fetching and carrying fever, and sowing more evil in its every footprint.

Residents of any major city in Europe or the United States would undoubtedly offer similar—if less evocative—descriptions of local slums or rundown neighborhoods where unemployment and crime are prevalent, drug abuse abounds, the roads and streetlights are not well maintained, and the schools are failing to equip students with the skills and knowledge necessary in the contemporary economy. Every major city has such neighborhoods, the ones that are "avoided by all decent people." Indeed, the urban riots in immigrant neighborhoods in Paris during 2005 are vivid reminders that decayed and despairing neighborhoods exist in even the most economically advanced states. Even first-time visitors to these cities learn from tourist guidebooks and the advice of concerned acquaintances to avoid these neighborhoods, at least after nightfall.

That pockets of enduring poverty and crime exist in American and European urban centers is, of course, well known. Apart from periodic and geographically limited attempts at urban renewal—essentially concentrated economic aid to finance the improvement of the public infrastructure or to subsidize the renovation of existing housing stock—the general approach taken by municipal governments has been containment. In other words, national and municipal governments try harder to limit the spillover of the spread of crime, drug abuse, and infrastructure erosion into neighborhoods where the problems are less significant (for example, wealthier or more politically active neighborhoods) than they do in eradicating the problems in the "black, dilapidated" streets of the worst neighborhoods.

This form of containment is reasonably successful, although urban riots do occur and no part of any city is ever completely free of criminal violence. This success is based upon the capacity of the national and municipal governments to deliver law enforcement/public safety services albeit unevenly in city neighborhoods. It is also based upon minimum levels of economic opportunity, which is, in turn, heavily dependent upon governments to maintain order necessary for daily commerce. Government assistance to the disadvantaged in the form of financial aid and access to health care is another factor.

Providing the necessary levels of economic opportunity and governmental assistance to the poorest neighborhoods and effective law enforcement/public safety services to all neighborhoods (but especially to the neighborhoods that are the poorest) can be difficult and expensive tasks, and the number of places where these tasks must be performed will only grow. Unfortunately, most of that growth will occur in cities and countries that are simply not well equipped to perform these tasks.

In 1950, there were 86 cities worldwide with more than 1 million inhabitants. By 2015, according to the United Nations Population Division, the number of cities with populations of 1 million or more will approach 600.[1] These larger cities and their suburban shantytowns, slums, and favelas will cover potentially hundreds of square miles—what the United Nations has aptly labeled large or very large urban agglomerations.[2]

Lagos, Nigeria, offers a prime example of the challenges of urban agglomerations, particularly within the fevered crescent. Nigeria's national and municipal governmental structures have consistently proven unable to deliver public services or to ensure public safety to the current urban population. The United States Agency for International Development's 2002 profile of cities in Nigeria indicated that Lagos and other large cities within the country are "very dangerous," particularly at night. Obviously, rampant high rates of crime are indicative of inadequate public safety services. Moreover, roughly

20 percent of the country's urban population lacks a clean water supply and almost as many lack adequate sewage support.[3] In 2002 this translated to more than 9 million Nigerians without reliable water and more than 7 million without sewage control.

By 2015, the population of Lagos will have doubled to more than 24 million, and other cities in Nigeria are projected for similarly dramatic population increases. It is hard to envision already brittle public services keeping pace with population changes of this magnitude. Indeed, the political and social discontent that is likely to accompany the population increases could very well cause public services to deteriorate in absolute terms. They could also result in many more millions of urban residents having to rely upon unclean drinking water and improvised, unhygienic methods of handling personal sewage. One result of such conditions is certain: high incidence of disease. In other words, social and economic pressures could result in cities like Lagos becoming even more dangerous and unhealthy.

Economic opportunities in such cities will not expand quickly enough to meet the needs of their burgeoning populations. There are no reliable unemployment statistics for Nigeria (in itself a sign of the governmental infrastructure problem that the state already faces), but extremely high underemployment rates can be inferred from the facts that 60 percent of the population has income below the poverty level and 70 percent is reportedly engaged in agriculture even though agriculture accounts for only 36 percent of Nigeria's GDP.[4] Thus there are not enough jobs in Nigerian cities today, and unless there are drastic changes, there will be even fewer relative to the huge population of potential job seekers in 2015 and 2050. In fact, the urban violence that occurs in cities such as Lagos due to simmering discontent and inadequate law enforcement/public safety services only makes the economic situation worse. Destruction of public infrastructure and private facilities does more than reduce the already limited capital stock; it also frightens off the potential investments that are essential to economic growth and job creation in the future.[5]

Reverse Quarantine?

If an analogy were to be drawn between a crime-ridden neighborhood in New York City or Paris to entire cities such as Lagos or Karachi, it would logically follow that the international community should impose a reverse quarantine upon itself.[6] It would contain the problems of the emerging megacities in the Lagos-Cairo-Karachi-Jakarta arc by sharply reducing all forms of interaction with them. While this approach works in a city—to the extent that the problems of decayed neighborhoods do not spill over into the other neighborhoods—it will not and cannot work at the global level.

Lagos again offers examples of how such a policy might be applied and why it would not be practical. In 1993, the U.S. Department of Transportation suspended commercial flights to Murtala Mohammad International Airport in Lagos due to concerns that the Nigerian government was not providing adequate security services for air traffic to and from the United States. The suspension lasted until 1999, but throughout the period of the suspension, other forms of interaction were unaffected.[7] During the six-year period of air traffic suspension, the United States maintained diplomatic relations with Nigeria; Nigerians were not excluded from applying for visas to the United States, and the United States and Nigeria continued to trade with each other. In fact, Nigeria was the sixth largest supplier of oil to the United States during that period.[8] This mixed picture will necessarily be typical of attempts to restrict relations and apply sanctions against other states. There are too many levels of interaction between states to think that this type of containment could work, and as economic globalization proceeds, the interactions will only become more irreversible.

In truth, neither Nigeria nor its capital can be put into reverse isolation by the United States. It is the largest and most powerful state in West Africa and the most populous country on the entire continent. In 2005 Nigeria's population was estimated to be 128 million.[9] If Nigeria were to collapse into chaos, the entire region would be destabilized.

Yet Lagos and the other major Nigerian cities are not unique in terms of the stresses that their governments will face as a result of urbanization. Roughly the same points could be made about most of the states in which other megacities are located. Egypt and Indonesia are clearly pivotal states in their respective regions; thus, the problems that emanate from Cairo, Jakarta, and other urban centers there cannot be contained through isolation. Pakistan is not as important strategically or economically as either Egypt or Indonesia, nor for that matter as three of the states on its borders (India, China, and Iran), but chaos there could well undermine efforts to combat terror and lead to serious tensions with India.

Further compounding the challenge that Lagos and other urban agglomerations will face is the phenomenon commonly called the "youth bulge." Today over half of the people of Egypt, Syria, Saudi Arabia, Iran, and Iraq are under the age of 25. Indonesia, the most populous Muslim nation, has a population of which 40 percent is under the age of 25. For Pakistan and

Afghanistan the percentage is even higher, roughly 62 percent. According to United Nations estimates, the number of youths (ages 0–24) in Africa will increase by about 60 percent between 2000 and 2015. After 2015 the rate of increase is expected to slow, but there will have been a net increase of 500 million people in the 0–24 age cohort in Africa by 2050. For Nigeria, the increase between 2000 and 2015 will be "only" 30 percent, but this will nevertheless represent an increase of about 25 million young people over 15 years.[10] Even where the proportion of young people is not dramatically increased, the absolute number of youthful job seekers in the cities of the less-developed world will grow—and will, in many cases, grow far beyond the capacity of the local economies to generate job opportunities and the capacity of the municipal infrastructure to provide needed schooling, public health services, sanitation, and housing.

The matter of sufficient job opportunities is an important factor because a society that has large numbers of unemployed youths is a society that is likely to experience high crime rates and violent disorder, as the riots in the immigrant neighborhoods of French cities in 2005 remind us.

The Rise of the "Feral City"?

Urban societies require extensive infrastructures: sewage, drinkable water, electricity, police, health care, education. These services, of course, are what make urban environments attractive. Cities offer (or at least are assumed by the rural poor to offer) opportunity, promise, and potential. Yet urban societies do not grow their own food, are highly susceptible to shifts in food and commodity supplies and prices, and can quickly become places of resource scarcity and deprivation—suffering from water shortages, unsanitary conditions, epidemics, and food deficits. Urban societies in the future might better be described as "large urban agglomerations"—to use the United Nations term—reflecting the fact that many cities are surrounded by suburban shantytowns, slums, and favelas that are often indistinguishable from the slums and favelas inside the official city boundaries.[11] These agglomerations can potentially extend over hundreds of square miles. Managing the provision of public services and expanding and then maintaining a complex, costly infrastructure of roads, hospitals and clinics, school buildings, water and sewage lines, and communication capabilities are challenges that all urban agglomerations face but that many outside North America and Europe will fail to meet.

It is too simplistic, nonetheless, to claim that overall population growth by itself leads to violent conflict. But a number of dynamically linked factors such as youth bulges, rapid shifts to urban areas, and infant mortality rates (on the negative side), as well as openness to international trade, some degree of technological capacity and sophistication within the society, and education that leads to employment (on the positive side) do bear important results. While it is too early to clearly project that demographic factors will lead to terrorist violence, this is an area ripe for research by social scientists and strategic analysts alike.

Some products of the failure to manage urban growth are, however, clearer. More often than not, it will be vast collections of wrecked foundations and ramshackle neighborhoods where the rule of law has been replaced by a Hobbesian anarchy in which the only security available is that which is attained through brutal, physically tangible muscle. Often that muscle will be at the service of corrupt elites or criminal organizations, both of which have stakes in the status quo. By virtue of their inadequate public health, water, and sanitation services, these cities will experience massive levels of disease and create pollution levels high enough to qualify as environmental disasters at the regional level. The consequences for future generations (the residents of the agglomerations in 2050) will be enormous. Air- and water-borne pollution in and around these cities could, like salt on a farmer's field, so foul the surrounding environments that they could become virtual barren zones. A vicious circle may thus emerge: the population of the affected cities will require productive use of the urban geography, yet restoring the area to productivity is too costly and the conditions only worsen while restoration is on hold.

Such urban nightmares are routinely envisioned in post-apocalyptic films and science fiction genres. Yet the nightmare already exists in isolated locations (the slums of Karachi and Lagos, for example), and as it spreads, it will contaminate cities that will—indeed must—remain globally connected. These cities, for all their anarchy and dysfunction, will retain direct and indirect commercial links to the rest of the world, and their inhabitants will be able to travel to other cities and will have access to the world's most modern communication and computing technologies.

These nightmarish, urban agglomerations will become, in effect, "feral cities."[12] Notably, Norman Myers described a similar phenomenon in 1990 in describing the "Termite Queen": in essence, urban centers, acting as a kind of super nest, attracting resources—both positive and negative—from rural centers, to include human capital and labor, skills, food, water, and raw materials.[13]

The feral city will be one of the more difficult security issues of the new century. The term itself is admittedly provocative, yet it represents a phenomenon already taking place throughout the globe. Examples include some of the notorious favelas in Rio de Janeiro and São Paulo and ungovernable areas in much of Karachi, Pakistan, and parts of greater Kinshasa in the Democratic Republic of Congo—locales where police have either never established an effective presence or have relinquished control. In some cases the choice to relinquish control may have been based on the most traditional of motives—corruption or indifference to conditions in minority communities. More disturbingly, in some cases the choice was based on the authorities' recognition that the costs of enforcing the law and guaranteeing public safety would be too great and might indeed simply be beyond the physical capacity of the municipal government. In such areas, social services are virtually nonexistent, and occupants have little or no access to even the most basic health and educational services, save for that provided by local nongovernment, often criminal, or even antigovernment organizations.

The more entrenched these nongovernment or antigovernment organizations become—as they will be as city and national governments fail to deliver services—the more difficult it will be for governments to reassert control. It is already the case in some cities. In certain Brazilian favelas and even in some UN-administered refugee camps that have virtually become cities, police forces have essentially chosen not even to attempt law enforcement.

In effect, these so-called feral parts of the city today have and perhaps entire feral cities tomorrow will have the ability to resist imposition of control and to wring concessions from the government—virtual exemptions from the standards and norms applied in the rest of the country. It may even be the case that these communities will be impervious to military action. If they were intent upon imposing control, military forces in the less developed states where megacities are mushrooming will have few technological advantages with respect to "close work" and will have no alternative to the kind of operations that will leave behind an immense field of rubble rather than a reclaimed and functioning population center.[14] Obviously there would be no political support domestically or internationally for such a military campaign.

There are, of course, issues that are more serious, even beyond criminality. Strains of existing or just emerging diseases will easily breed and mutate in the feral city. And, while as of this writing the fear of a global Severe Acute Respiratory Syndrome (SARS) outbreak seems to have largely diminished, the reasons for the infectious disease's demise in 2003 may have had more to do with the change of seasons than with the efforts of health workers to combat the disease.[15] It is nevertheless true that in the case of SARS, the existence of the disease was rapidly identified, the point of origin speedily traced, and a medical offensive quickly mounted.

Had such a disease originated in a feral city, the processes of determining that a new outbreak had occurred, identifying the nature of the disease, and locating its sources of contagion would have been substantially delayed (very likely to the point where international transmission would become possible). Further, even if the disease were identified early, actually mounting an effective medical and public health response would be extremely complicated due to the inadequate municipal infrastructure and the volatility of the social climate.

The late 2004–early 2005 outbreak of the Marburg virus in Angola may be a harbinger of the kinds of problems that will encountered with disease in the future. In April 2005, the United Nations' World Health Organization (WHO) dispatched teams of experts to contain the virus and treat its victims. But the Angola government then announced that the outbreak actually had started in October 2004. Posthumous tests conducted by WHO in March 2005 confirmed this.[16] Not only was the medical response delayed by Angola's technical incapacity to identify public health threats quickly, but the government either failed or was unable to inform the public about the nature of the response. As a result, WHO teams were attacked by local residents and had to be withdrawn. A hospital operated by Médecins Sans Frontières in which Marburg victims were being treated also had to be closed temporarily due to threats of violence.[17]

Increasingly, given our webs of globalized interconnectivity, the world cannot afford to let six months or even six days elapse between the initial outbreak of a highly contagious and deadly disease and its identification and quantification. The United States has a public health reporting system that is designed to identify pathogens rapidly, and that system has been substantially upgraded as part of the effort to protect the country against bioterrorism, but in many parts of the world the threat is natural, and there are no equivalent public health systems.

Large cities already place significant environmental stresses on their local and regional environments. Nowhere are these problems more pronounced than in coastal metropolises. Even modern cities that invest in pollution controls, sanitation, and waste-processing systems put substantial stress on local environments. Fast-growing urban agglomerations in parts of the world where pollution and environmental systems are undeveloped will have the potential to poison coastlines, watersheds, and river systems throughout their respective regions.[18] Where the governments do not operate environmental protection and remediation programs, as most will not, the result will be a vicious cycle. The longer there are no effective sanitation and recycling systems, the worse the environmental problem will become. Given the large number of challenges that governments in the fevered crescent will face, it is likely that pollution control will not have a high priority. Thus the cycle may stay vicious for a considerable period of time.

Major cities are already trying to contend with black market activity that ranges from evading legal fees, dues, and taxes to trafficking in illegal and banned materials. Black marketeers in an undergoverned city would have virtual carte blanche to ship or receive such materials to or from a global audience.[19]

Yet as serious as these transnational issues are, a further threat is far more dangerous. Not only does the potentially anarchic nature of under-governed cities make them an attractive location for criminal groups. It may also make them useful havens for certain types of terrorist activities—specifically, fund-raising, recruitment, weapons acquisition (including perhaps weapons of mass destruction), and temporary "safe havening." Further, the existence of international transportation nodes in these cities will enable terrorist groups to "export" terrorism to the rest of the world.

Feral cities do not represent merely a sociological or urban planning issue; they present unique security challenges as well. Their very size and density make them natural havens for hostile nonstate actors, ranging from small cells of terrorists to large paramilitary forces and militias. History indicates that should such a group take hostages (as they did in Beirut in the 1970s, in Teheran in 1979–1980, and more recently in post-sovereignty Iraq), successful rescue is not likely.[20] Operations in such environments tend to be manpower intensive, and limiting noncombatant casualties can be extraordinarily difficult. The defense of the Warsaw ghetto in World War II suggests how costly a conventional military assault can be in such an urban environment.

Identifying Feral Cities

If the world is to do anything about the phenomenon, other than observe and bemoan it, the first step is to recognize which urban agglomerations are already undergoverned or are at the risk of becoming feral. The most reliable indicators revolve around one theme—the provision of public services, including public safety and law enforcement and the availability of alternatives to reliance upon public services; for example, the kind provided by the private sector economy in the form of jobs, nongovernment schools, private security forces. Any city in which these services are not provided to substantial proportions of the population is at risk. The risks to such a city are sharply increased when its population is growing at a fast and sustained pace.

Many cities, of course, have neighborhoods or sectors that are underserved, and distinguishing between functional cities with disadvantaged neighborhoods and feral cities is not a simple matter. Moreover, the task is complicated by the fact that the national governments of states are not likely to willingly acknowledge that they have lost control over major urban centers inside their border. Admitting such a fact would be tantamount to declaring political bankruptcy and would, moreover, serve no practical purpose until such time as there was an institution that was capable of doing what the national government had failed to do—provide services to an unruly metropolis. A state's denial will do more than complicate the analytical task of identifying feral cities; it will present an imposing roadblock to the mobilization of collective international action to improve the situation.

Mexico City exhibits some of the characteristics of a feral city. It is one of the largest urban agglomerations in the world, and it has recently been described as an urban nightmare. Its air is so polluted that it is routinely rated medically as unfit to breathe. There are square miles of slums, often without sewage or running water. Serious crime has doubled over the past three to four years; it is estimated that 15.5 million assaults now occur every year in Mexico City. Carjacking and taxi-jacking have reached such epidemic proportions that visitors are now officially warned not to use the cabs. The Mexico City police department has 91,000 officers—more men than the Canadian army—but graft and corruption on the force are rampant and on the rise. According to Mexican senator Adolfo Zinser, police officers themselves directly contribute to the city's crime statistics: "In the morning they are policemen. In the afternoon they're crooks." (In Sierra Leone and some other West African countries, this day-night alternation of roles is so ingrained that members of the army have earned the sobriquet *sobels*, which stands for "soldiers by day, rebels by night.") Mexico City's judicial system is equally corrupt. Not surprisingly, these aspects of life in Mexico City have reduced the willingness of foreign investors to send money or representatives there.[21]

Johannesburg offers another example of a city at risk of going feral. While many recognize South Africa as the superpower on the continent, few are disposed to acknowledge that Johannesburg is a city with serious issues. That the South African stock exchange moved out of Johannesburg and into the northern suburb of Sandton in the early twenty-first century was perhaps just the first indicator of serious trouble afoot. As one financial analyst phrased it for the authors in a confidential e-mail:

> The Johannesburg Stock Exchange (JSE) moved to Sandton in September 2001. The main reason was a practical one: after the introduction of on-line trading there was no longer a need for a central trading floor, which was the key feature of the city-centre building. The financial "district" had already mostly migrated to Sandton, which had by then become the new financial heart of the country. This meant that the JSE's key clients—fund managers, investment houses, merchant bankers, etc.—were all in and around Sandton. There is no doubt that unacceptable levels of crime and the general decay of central Johannesburg significantly contributed to the general drift to Sandton, as well as the upmarket infrastructure and availability of the right shops, services, restaurants, hotels, etc. As a tangential thought—the JSE's key relationship with the mining houses, all of whom were splendidly situated in grand buildings in central Johannesburg, also weakened as the emphasis shifted to global investment dominated by more "faceless" institutions. SA's largest and most successful bank, Standard, made a conscious and much discussed decision to remain in central Johannesburg and thereby to help anchor plans for urban renewal. As you saw, inner city renewal has a long way to go, but it is unquestionably a process that has commenced. However, it is likely that Sandton will remain the financial "capital," and other activities, including the civil service or inner city residential renewal, will drive the regeneration of Johannesburg centre.

As with many South African cities, police in Johannesburg have been waging a desperate war for control, and it is not clear if they will win. While tourist and official government documents proclaim that security has improved overall in Johannesburg (thanks in part to the installation of a wide-network video surveillance system), the South African government actually stopped issuing crime statistics in July 2000—only to resume a year later in releasing statistics with different categories. No matter what the distinctions, though, the news remains unpleasant: one in three people robbed in

2003, murder rates in the greater metro area of 60 per 100,000 (three times that of America's most dangerous cities), and an environment where businesses regularly cite crime as a major obstacle to growth.[22]

Massive in relative sprawl, with only 3.2 million official residents, Johannesburg suffers more than 5,000 murders a year and twice as many rapes—far above the "average" for a city of such size. Over the last several years, investors and major industry have, like the stock exchange, fled the city. Many of the major buildings of the Central Business District (including the once fashionable—even Bohemian—section known as Hill Brow) have been abandoned and are now homes to squatters and overcrowded tenements. At night, residents are advised to remain in their homes. Tourism has dried up, and conventions, once a common source of revenue, are now hosted elsewhere in the country.

The city also suffers from high rates of air pollution, primarily from vehicle exhaust, but also from numerous cooking and heating systems that rely on open fires and the use of coal as fuel. Johannesburg's two rivers are also considered "unsafe." Sources of river pollution consist primarily of untreated human waste and chemicals leaching from piles of mining dross. Mining has also contaminated much of the soil in the vicinity. Johannesburg's problems are exacerbated by the AIDS epidemic. Nationally, as many as 25 percent of the population—and 90 percent of some units in the army—is HIV positive.[23] Pessimistic assessments from the World Bank further suggest that, if left unchecked, the HIV/AIDS pandemic has the potential to collapse the South African economy within four decades.[24] Such an event would be devastating for the continent. Johannesburg's province produces 36.3 percent of the Republic of South Africa's gross domestic product and 10 percent of the overall gross domestic product of all sub-Saharan African economies.[25]

It would be premature, nonetheless, to project that Mexico City and Johannesburg will necessarily become feral cities. In the case of Mexico City, police corruption has been an aspect of city life for decades.[26] The transition from one political party to two and a reduction in public sector employment may be exerting a temporarily adverse impact on the city but should promote economic growth and political stability over the long run. In the case of Johannesburg, the South African government has most definitely not given up on trying to revive what was once an industrial and economic showplace. Both states possess dedicated men and women who are adamant about doing something to eliminate corruption, clean the environment, and improve the lives of their peoples. Yet it is appropriate to sound a note of caution: the trends in both examples are not aimed in a positive direction.

Going Feral

While Johannesburg and Mexico City clearly show signs of strain under burgeoning populations and inadequate infrastructures, these cities remain more promisingly resilient than many others. Nairobi illustrates the difficult challenges that a less-resilient city faces.

Sadly, the engine fueling this ongoing decay in Kenya stems from the rampant corruption of government officials and politicians, who often refuse to assist honestly in development or to refrain from personal enrichment. Although British ambassadors to Kenya in the past normally have been reticent to express direct criticism of government failures, High Commissioner Edward Clay, in a speech to the British Business Association of Kenya in 2004, was quite blunt:

> We never expected corruption to be vanquished overnight. We all implicitly recognized that some would be carried over to the new era [after the time of Daniel arap Moi]. We hoped it would not be rammed in our faces. But it has. Evidently, the practitioners now in government have the arrogance, greed, and perhaps a desperate sense of panic to lead them to eat like gluttons. They may expect we shall not see, or notice, or forgive them a bit of gluttony because they profess to like OXFAM lunches. But they can hardly expect us not to care when their gluttony causes them to vomit all over our shoes. Do they really expect us to ignore the lurid and mostly accurate details conveyed in the commendably free media and pursued by a properly curious Parliament?[27]

To be sure, Clay's remarks spurred howls of indignation from the government. Yet, according to a World Bank study, exorbitant funds are spent annually on bribes in Kenya. Corruption allegedly accounts for 8 percent of its gross domestic product. Even more astonishing in terms of disparity, estimates claim that Kenyan members of Parliament award themselves an average of $169,625 a year in salaries and allowances while the average Kenyan income is $400 a year.[28] (This is virtually the same pay given to members of the Congress of the United States; but the average American's income is about $40,000. If the Kenyan scale were applied to the United States, each Congressman and Senator would be paid about $2 million annually.)

In 2005, High Commissioner Clay apologized—with a twist. Claiming regret for the "moderation" of his earlier language, he said that he had underestimated the scale of the looting and failed to speak out earlier, for which the Kenyan government subsequently referred to him as an "incorrigible liar." Despite this counteraccusation, John Githongo, appointed by President Mwai Kibaki to root out corruption, resigned from office and fled Kenya, fearing for his life. The United States, doubting the Kenyan government's credibility, abruptly canceled a $2.5 million aid package to assist in rooting out corruption. Clay subsequently handed over a dossier detailing 20 corruption scandals involving ministers. According to the American ambassador, William Bellamy, the money that disappeared in these cases could have provided funding for every HIV-positive Kenyan in the country for the next decade.[29]

What is most tragic, of course, is that such human actions are more controllable than environmental, demographic, or pandemic circumstances that often propel peoples into serious decline. The gross and intentional rape of a people by its own leaders is an unforgivable injustice. Extreme comparisons admittedly, Clay makes the following blunt comparisons:

> The value of the [Kenyan Shilling] Sh15 billion corrupt deals originated and negotiated under the present government would also: Buy [a fleet of] Mercedes S350s. Keep your eyes open for them and their drivers (or more interesting, passengers); Fund the construction of 15,000 odd new classrooms (just under half the Ministry of Education says it needs). But I doubt it's worth your trouble trying to spot them. At the lower end of the scale of opportunity costs, Sh1 billion would buy 5 million double-size treated bednets. Their availability would save 65,000 child lives lost to malaria. That same Sh1 billion is worth half the pre-tax profit made last year by Kenyan Airways, "the Pride of Africa"; Or just under the tax (Sh1.2 billion) paid by one of its most successful exporters; Enough to buy the vaccines to immunize 21,740,000 children. If they funded that in somewhere needy (say, S. Sudan) Kenya could join the ranks of the donors—a first in Africa. Or enough to feed a hot lunch to 712,000 school children for a year. Put another way, some officers of this Government have helped squander many times more than Sh1 billion. We are talking of corruption worth 15 times as much initiated in the last 18 months.[30]

Ironically, longtime opposition leader Mwai Kibaki ousted Daniel arap Moi in presidential elections in 2003 on an avowed anticorruption platform. Moi, through a systematic and practiced corrupt regime, made Kenyans progressively poorer for decades. Kibaki came to power promising to root out corruption and to get the state "on track." Sadly, his health declined quickly, and his ability to control his own ministers came into question. The anticorruption Berlin-based watch group Transparency International, nevertheless, "upgraded" Kenya's corruption rating in 2004 from "highly acute" to merely "rampant."[31] Curiously, this marginally improved rating actually prompted some Kenyans to question why foreign investors were not flocking back to set up new ventures.

Yet the problem for Kenya, of course, is not just corruption. The lethal combination of government corruption, declining infrastructure, and swelling populations fueled increasingly negative consequences. Modern Nairobi represents the central symbol of this fearful decline, one that cannot be blamed simply on colonialism's imperialist legacy. To the contrary:

> Modern Nairobi is a condemnation of independence. The slums girdling the city center are swamps of hopelessness. The streets and sidewalks are falling apart, prolonged power failures plunge entire neighborhoods into almost nightly blackouts. Muggings, murders, and carjackings are so common they have to be spectacular to make the front pages of the daily newspapers, and with tourism declining, security service is probably the only growth industry left in the country. Almost every restaurant and office building in the capital hire *askaris* [security guards] as protection against criminal invasions.
>
> Old hands bemoan Kenya's decay, telling nostalgic tales about a nation that once seemed exempt from the social, economic, and political dysfunctions plaguing the rest of sub-Saharan Africa. In some ways it still is. At least it's been spared the hideous genocidal conflict that turned Rwanda into a mass graveyard, the famines that starved millions in Ethiopia, the intractable civil wars that have brought chaos to Somalia, Sierra Leone, the Congo, and Sudan. Nevertheless, an exploding population (from about 8.3 million at independence in 1963 to more than 30 million today) has worked hand in hand with the kleptocratic regime . . . to slowly but inexorably unravel Kenya's social fabric. Tribal chieftains calling themselves ministers of parliament stay in power by playing off ancient rivalries between Kikuyu and Luo, Turkana and Samburu, Kamba and Mbere, plundering the public treasury, and leaving the masses to struggle for the scraps. Some, the more vigorous and angry, aren't willing to struggle and aren't interested in scraps and take whatever they can lay their hands on, often with vio-

lence. "Don't go out at night," the pretty front desk clerk at the Norfolk Hotel warned us. "Thugs in town, bandits in the countryside."[32]

Increasingly, urban centers have become magnets for jobs, education, and health care as well as locales rampant with crime, competition for limited resources, and tensions among citizens. Increased consumption within cities also impacts rural environments; in 1990, for example, Norman Myers stressed in addressing "Supercities" that the major cause of deforestation in rural Kenya was from the widespread conversion of wood to charcoal for sale in urban centers.[33]

Moreover, although perhaps empirically difficult to prove as either a consequence or precondition of the nation-state's fragility, a senior official of an international organization working in Nairobi declared to one of the authors, P. H. Liotta, without hesitation, that Kenyans are prone to a "culture of violence." Without question, there has also been a general sense of dismay and disappointment at the relative lack of progress made by Moi's successor, Kibaki. Often, moments after engaging in general discussion, Kenyans expressed bitter disappointment—indeed resentment—at the perceived failure of Kibaki to effect change. "Nothing . . . he's done nothing" was a common refrain.

Liotta also personally encountered disturbing instances of Kenya's and Nairobi's general disorder through a series of observed or related incidents. Granted, such evidence is highly subjective; it does relate, nonetheless, to cited examples of the decaying condition of the state and the region. These observations became immediately apparent when he was physically prevented from walking on the streets of Nairobi. The hotel doorman, Caleb, firmly insisted, "I'm sorry, sir. Guests just don't do that." While Nairobi is hardly the only city in which hotel guests are warned against wandering in certain neighborhoods, in this case the risk of crime and violence was so great (and the absence of public safety and law enforcement protection so absolute) that the warning amounted to virtual protective custody inside the hotel.

While there were sections of Nairobi of undeniable beauty, much of the city and its outlying regions seemed overused and exhausted. Due to the higher altitude of 1,660 meters (5,460 feet), the high charcoal burn rate, and traffic belching exhaust fumes, the atmosphere is dense, almost impenetrable with gray-black fog mornings. The streets are jammed with traffic, especially the ever-present and always dangerous *matatu* public vehicles.[34] Always overcrowded to the bursting point, and always driven by seemingly lunatic drivers, these fragile vehicles teeter in and out of asynchronous traffic chaos, heading toward some inevitable disaster. The first serious automobile accident Liotta witnessed was on leaving the residential district of Karen (formerly the writer Isak Dinesen's/Karen Blixen's estate) and coming across a *matatu* flipped completely on its back and nose down in a gulley. Notably, most of the Kenyans on the scene commented noisily to each other on how dangerous this *matatu* driver was compared with others.

But evidence of violent leanings, of course, must go far beyond merely taking relish at reckless drivers. The evidence was not lacking. Liotta was told constantly, for example, not to interfere at the scene of a crime. The common explanation was that police were uniformly corrupt and more interested in taking bribes for beer than in maintaining any sense of order. One individual related how recently a purse thief was literally "collared" by an enraged mob at the very scene of the crime; he was seized moments after the theft, bound, and, with a rubber tire set around his torso, set aflame. Another incident, in which police chose not to intervene, involved the thugs of a real estate developer who were sent to clear squatters off his property. In this case, the squatter women alone attacked the thugs, doused them in kerosene, and set them on fire. The squatters remained.

Perhaps the most personal and disturbing incident the author encountered came while visiting the home of a senior official in an exclusive residential neighborhood not far from the newly constructed U.S. embassy. (The previous embassy was destroyed by a terrorist bombing in August 1998. An architect who had worked on other embassies in the country allegedly claimed that the new building—which looks like nothing other than a maximum security prison—could withstand a nuclear impact.) Winding through the switchbacks that gently slope up the hillsides of rows upon rows of coffee trees, the official remarked, "We never take these roads at night. Too dangerous. Thugs . . . kids, really . . . step out of the coffee rows with AK-47s or pistols planted square in your face. They mean to rob you blind or hijack you. They'll shoot you if you resist. They still might shoot you if you don't."

Topping a ridge, we looked across a minor depression to his neighborhood. He proudly declared that he loved to watch eagles soar up and down this minor valley during the day. Yet across on the other slope the entire hillside had been deforested. His explanation was clear: "This makes gangs moving up from the slums on raids far more noticeable. Easier to spot." His remarks were even more startling given that walls of concrete surrounding the entire residential section were at least four meters high in many sections.

Upon arriving at his home, he and Liotta were greeted by his askari and one house assistant. The home was a modest English cottage, which snugly accommodated him, his wife, and their two young children. It was situated on nearly five acres of land, an almost unthinkable luxury for many Kenyans. Yet he described neighborhood break-ins where weapons fire was exchanged, spilling over into neighboring resident properties. On more than one occasion, their own house had been targeted, though without shots being fired.

He related one specific and harrowing break-in. The exact details of the incident were revealed in retrospect, after a young domestic was interrogated following the incident.

The domestic revealed that she had been "dating" a resident of Kenya for less than two weeks. He repeatedly asked her about the residence she worked at; the hours when security was and was not present; the state and location of alarm systems on premises. It also appeared that he beat her. The official and family admitted they had seen signs of domestic violence but believed her explanation that she had been mugged.[35]

The night of the break-in was well orchestrated. Four or five thugs targeted the one door without sensor alarms and smashed the locks on steel French doors with sledgehammers and entered the home. The official and his family, fortunately awakened by the fracas, had barricaded themselves in the home's "safe zone," behind a gridded security gate. (Although perhaps odd for some to accept, Liotta regularly saw families "lock" themselves behind barriers when retiring to sleeping quarters for the night, both in South Africa and Kenya.) The official, nonetheless, furious and a bit foolish, stood behind the barrier and heard the lead planner of the break-in say repeatedly with lethal hatred four precise words as he entered the house: "We will kill you."

The official was able to remotely alert security forces, which arrived several minutes later. The thieves took little more than a stereo system, cameras, and personal items. They fled as the security backup team arrived.

The experience itself lingered, nonetheless, raw and unnerving. The official remembers looking directly at the thief and hearing his words, while his wife, crying in terror, huddled in the bedroom, hugging their children.

Liotta's personal experiences reminded us of one of the most striking (and, by Robert Kaplan's own admission to us, overlooked) passages from the somewhat hyperbolic essay "The Coming Anarchy":

> Think of a stretch limo in the potholed streets of New York City, where
> homeless beggars live. Inside the limo are the air-conditioned post-

industrial regions of North America, Europe, the emerging Pacific Rim, and a few other isolated places, with their trade summitry and computer-information highways. Outside is the rest of mankind, going in a completely different direction. We are entering a bifurcated world. Part of the globe is inhabited by Hegel's and Fukuyama's Last Man, healthy, well fed, and pampered by technology. The other, larger, part is inhabited by Hobbes's First Man, condemned to a life that is "poor, nasty, brutish, and short." Although both parts will be threatened by environmental stress, the Last Man will be able to master it; the First Man will not.

The Last Man will adjust to the loss of underground water tables in the western United States. He will build dikes to save Cape Hatteras and the Chesapeake beaches from rising sea levels, even as the Maldive Islands, off the coast of India, sink into oblivion, and the shorelines of Egypt, Bangladesh, and Southeast Asia recede, driving tens of millions of people inland where there is no room for them, and thus sharpening ethnic divisions.[36]

Kenya, of course, is not beyond hope. Nor is it a state without hope. One need only look at Somalia for the identity of a failed state, or to Zimbabwe for a state blessed with resources but left rudderless under the hopeless "leadership" of Robert Mugabe. But Kenya is a state foundering in quicksand, with precious few grains of sand left in the hourglass.

The problem does not just reside in cities; to the contrary, the problems are as exacerbated in remote rural regions. Again, during a recent trip to Africa, a colleague from Uganda reminded Liotta of an image Richard Leakey often showed to audiences in Europe and North America: a slide photograph of a striking gazelle in the foreground against a backdrop of classic African nature. Leakey's point was blunt: "To you, this gazelle is the classic beauty of the landscape. This is Africa. To the African, this gazelle means food. This is Africa." The similar reality exists for Kenya, and will remain. As Philip Caputo perhaps too bluntly describes it:

> That's the difference between the West and here. In the West, you have time to do things like observe lions and measure their skulls. Here, everyone is just trying to survive, day to day". . . . [H]er remarks awakened memories of the things I'd seen in southern Sudan—boys with legs blown off by land mines, a mission church blasted by a Sudanese air force cluster bomb, a mother who had walked through the bush for six days to bring her child, feverish with malaria, to the nearest

clinic. . . . Tsavo and the Serengeti are what tourists—and writers and scientists—want to see of Africa, but the real Africa is millions upon millions of people suffering through dismal poverty, AIDS, malaria, drought, famine, utterly corrupt regimes, overcrowded cities, intractable civil wars. . . . If Thoreau was right, that in wilderness we do find our salvation, then I guess we are damned. All we can do is mourn the lost wonder and wildness of the world and fight rear-guard actions to save what's left from ourselves. It isn't the free market that's at fault, or socialism or industrialism or any other ism; there are too many of us.[37]

The paradox, of course, is that Kenya's strength, its one great resource, is its people. High Commissioner Clay emphasized this in his original blistering critique of 2004, claiming:

Kenya is not a rich country in terms of large oil deposits, diamonds or some other buffer which might featherbed a thorough-going culture of corruption. What it chiefly has is its people—their intelligence, work ethic, education, entrepreneurial and other skills. That is what we mean when we talk of Kenya's potential ability to regain its diminishing economic and other leadership in the region. But these assets will be lost if they are not managed, rewarded well and properly led. One day we may wake up at the end of this gigantic looting spree to find Kenya's potential is all behind us and it is a land of lost opportunity.[38]

Clay's cautionary words cannot be dismissed lightly. Indeed, the severe pressures imposed on Kenya have, more often than not, been self-imposed. While true irony may lie in the belief some hold that Kenya is a more productive model of success than many states in East Africa, its rapid population growth (as high as 4.1 percent per annum, by some estimates—resulting in the doubling of population every 17 years) is a crippling reality.[39]

While expectations might suggest that population levels in Africa (where humans have resided longer than anywhere else) would have leveled off some time ago, the introduction of new crops from the West, preventive medicine and vaccinations, control of malaria and other endemic diseases, and new agricultural methods (including those rising from the "Green Revolution" of the 1960s) partially explain why some areas are now habitable that were formerly no-man's-lands throughout the continent.[40] Yet continued lack of attention, direction, and resources can easily lead a city and an entire region into feral conditions that pose risk to their populations and will threaten, in one way or another, most distant parts of the globe. The next section is a disturbing illustration of one place where this has clearly occurred.

The Prototypical Feral City

Thus far, we have considered examples of cities that have demonstrated one or more aspects of feral cities, including the inability of the governmental authorities to control the streets after dark. Lagos and Johannesburg, in particular, prove worth considering because both hint at the interconnectedness that major cities—even feral cities—have and will retain with the United States and the rest of the world.

At the close of this chapter we present a snapshot of a particular aspect of Karachi that is another prototype of a megacity. Karachi is, for important strategic reasons, the prototypical *connected* feral city. First, the government of Pakistan is a critical piece in the effort to confront terrorism, although its criticality is as much a function of its ability to cause trouble as its capacity for suppressing terrorist groups and interdicting terrorist operations. Pakistan has a history of promoting terrorism (through support for the Taliban in Afghanistan and for Muslim extremists in Kashmir and India proper). Nevertheless, the United States and the West in general recognize that without Pakistan's compliance if not enthusiastic commitment, the global war on terror, especially Islamist terror, will be considerably more arduous. Much the same can be said for Pakistan's nuclear weapons program—the country may be most important due to its ability to cause trouble—and the very existence of the program is another sign of Pakistan's strategic importance. Pakistan has a history of having contributed to nuclear proliferation through illegal weapons sales and technology exports. Its apparent commitment to nuclear controls, if it is both sincere and effectively implemented, may be an important element of the global effort to limit the spread of weapons of mass destruction.

Pakistan's commercial interactions with the rest of the world are economically insignificant. Its principal exports are widely available commodities: textiles, rice, and leather.[41] There would, therefore, be no economic downsides to restricting trade and other interactions with Karachi. (This was not the case with Nigeria, whose oil exports are economically significant.) However, any attempt by the international community to restrict interactions with Karachi would likely spur a number of undesirable responses by the Pakistani government. Pakistan could, for example, threaten to back out of its nonproliferation and antiterror commitments as a bargaining chip for the restoration of full communications and transportation links with Karachi. Under such conditions, the West would find it impossible to maintain a serious economic interdiction of Pakistan.

It is estimated that more than half (50 percent) of Karachi's population of 10–15 million resides in shantytowns, communities where virtually no public services are provided.[42] The shantytowns themselves are illegal, and their enduring existence is standing testimony to the inability of the government to enforce its writ. As to the public services being delivered to the population of Karachi, it is estimated that only 60 percent of the garbage created by 10–15 million people is collected and only 14 percent of the sewage that the city and its shantytowns create is treated. Air pollution in the city is estimated to be 20 times worse than the maximum level recommended by the United Nations.[43] These obviously unhealthy, disease-friendly conditions are a direct result of the incapacity of the national and municipal governments to deliver services. Making matters worse, the United Nations Office for the Coordination of Humanitarian Affairs estimates that approximately 600 million gallons of water would be required to meet the needs of Karachi's legal and illegal residents, but the city currently gets only two-thirds of that amount due largely to the absence of investment in new public water systems and disrepair of the existing infrastructure.[44]

Law enforcement and public safety are other services in scant supply in Karachi and indeed throughout the country. Complicating the dire public health situation created by untreated sewage, uncollected garbage, and air pollution is the fact that Pakistan's medical professionals have been targeted for violence and the state has been unable to protect them. Since 1997, 270 physicians, most based in Karachi, have been murdered in the country.[45] Most of the victims were Shiites, apparently targeted because of their religious affiliation by Sunni terrorists. But the important points with respect to law enforcement and public safety is that the government has been unable to conserve a scarce resource (physicians) for which the city's unhealthy environment has created a special and critical demand. The physicians are, in fact, crucial to helping the city's residents deal with the diseases and wounds that the city's other incapacities help to create.

Warning Signs

While, admittedly, there are real dangers in anecdotes, there are some benefits as well in the illustrative aspects that anecdotes reveal. Consider, for example, the single incident related to us by a colleague in Kenya regarding a backpacking trip that he and several schoolmates had made years earlier in West Africa. While traveling through the Muslim-dominated northern city of Kano, Nigeria, they stopped at a roadside café for lunch. Noticing that the innkeeper brought some soft drinks to several children who were playing nearby, the backpackers—in an altruistic moment—decided to chip in and buy the children a roast chicken.

When the waiter took the order out to the roadside for the children to eat, the scene became suddenly transformed. Their eyes widened into moons of hunger, and collectively and literally they leapt on the meat. Rationally, one would think, the children would divide the apportionment of the food equitably amongst themselves, with each receiving a "fair" share. This, of course, is exactly what did not happen. Rather than thinking, they reacted with need. The children turned on each other, kicking and biting, and the scene quickly became one of desperate violence. The chicken was torn apart and most fell into the dirt and was batted away, ruined. The children continued to fight with each other, then moved on, still hungry.

The point of the anecdote, we would argue, aside from its human tragedy, is that as complex aspects tend to accumulate, responses and actions are not always as expected. Complex dynamics that impact security—pandemics, lack of resources, declining food access and availability, increased urbanization, competition for decreased opportunity—can produce violent, and certainly chaotic, responses.

The scientific debate regarding the certainty of outcomes for issues regarding human security and environmental impact rages on. The debate itself, in its best forms, ought to necessarily impact future policy decisions, though that has not always proved true in the past.

One of the most compelling cases, nonetheless, stems from the 1994 genocide in Rwanda. Tragically, this specific instance of mass killing was different only in the scale of slaughter that occurred—it ranks as one of the worst genocides on record.[46] Other instances of killing between Hutus and Tutsi have occurred in both Rwanda and Burundi throughout the twentieth and twenty-first centuries. Even today in Rwanda—where identity cards are now banned that, before 1994, identified citizens as Hutu or Tutsi—conditions are little better than they were in 1994 and tensions remain high. In 1994, however, as many as 1 million people died during the 100 days of genocide. No one will ever know the exact number.

Doubtless, the brutal colonial legacy of European colonizers, particularly the Belgians (who originally imposed the practice of ethnic identity cards) played a significant role in creating these tensions. Hutus are generally be-

lieved to have come from the south and west and to have settled Rwanda and
Burundi first; Tutsis are believed to be a Nilotic people from the north and
east, who arrived in central sub-Saharan Africa after the Hutus, yet became
"overlords" of the Hutu. Hutus (numbering 85 percent of Rwanda's population) are primarily farmers; allegedly, Hutus are shorter, stockier, flat-nosed,
and thick-lipped. Tutsis are primarily pastoralists; allegedly, Tutsis are taller,
slender, pale-skinned, thin-lipped and supposedly more European or "Ham-
itic" in appearance. Belgian colonizers actively promoted these alleged differences, particularly in promoting Tutsi domination over Hutu. Yet, as with
so many conflicts often labeled "ethnic conflicts," the issue of ethnicity is
problematic. (Admittedly, the term *genocide* only aggravates this perception
of ethnic difference.) Aside from the levels of intermarriage between Hutus
and Tutsis, there is no clean distinction between the two groups. Indeed, as
Diamond notes, the usual interpretations of ethnic cleansing in Rwanda are
"wrong, incomplete, or oversimplified."[47]

The tragedy of Rwanda, rather, can be expressed as a horrific example
of the economist and demographer Thomas Robert Malthus's 1798 work in
which he suggested that human population (which grows exponentially)
would outpace food production (which increases only arithmetically). Certainly, thanks to improved technology and agricultural methods, this has not
occurred on a massive scale despite the swelling human population of the
twentieth century. Indeed, even in Bangladesh (with relatively few killings
since the massive slaughter that occurred in 1971), as well as the Nether-
lands and Belgium—all states with denser populations than Rwanda—relative peace and progress have been maintained. Population stress, as one of
any number of complex influences we emphasize here, can nonetheless lead
to violent outcomes.

Rwanda, known as the land of "des Mille Collines"—the thousand hills—
is three times more densely populated than Africa's most populated state
(Nigeria) and 10 times more populated than neighboring Tanzania. Rwanda's problems, nonetheless, were not simply isolated to issues of population
pressure. According to Michael Renner, "In Rwanda, population growth and
limited economic opportunities put immense pressure on the land. Over-
cultivation diminished soil fertility, cutting grain harvests by 32 percent
between 1990 and 1993. The resulting economic desperation allowed Hutu
extremists to play up ethnic tensions, culminating in a murderous 1994 ram-
page that led to hundreds of thousands of civilian deaths."[48]

Notably, Rwandans themselves tend to confirm these pressures. Rather
than placing an emphasis on ethnic differences, the conflictual state came
down to simple explanation:

It is not rare, even today, to hear Rwandans argue that a war is necessary to wipe out an excess of population and to bring numbers into
line with available land resources. . . . The decision to kill was of course
made by politicians, for political reasons. But at least part of the reason
why it was carried out so thoroughly by the ordinary rank-and-file in
their *ingo* [family compound] was feeling that there were too many
people on too little land, and that with a reduction in their numbers,
there would be more for the survivors.[49]

There is also evidence that despite the Hutu extremist belief that eliminating
roughly 15 percent of the Tutsi overall Rwandan population would lead to
greater access and opportunity for the survivors, the reality was more bleak.
As Diamond illustrates in the case of Kanama in Rwanda, drawing exclusively on the work of Belgian economists Catherine André and Jean-Philippe
Platteau, Hutus turned to killing Hutus in a rural region where there were
few Tutsi and the Tutsi population could not, therefore, be blamed for the
overall lack of access, opportunity, and availability of critical resources.[50]

The tragedy of Rwanda, as may be the future tragedy of many rural locales
in the fevered crescent of the future, came down to the basic struggle of the
"haves" versus the "wants." As Gérard Prunier, a French specialist on East
Africa, observed, echoing the thoughts and true sentiments on survivors of
the Rwandan tragedy: "All these people who were about to be killed had land
and at times cows. And somebody had to have these lands and those cows
after the owners were dead. In a poor and increasingly overpopulated country this was not a negligible incentive. . . . The people whose children had to
walk barefoot to school killed the people who could buy shoes for theirs."[51]

Addressing Ferality

It should come as no surprise that massive cities in most of the world are at
far greater risk of becoming feral than are those in more developed states
such as Mexico and the Republic of South Africa. Mexico, for all its problems, has an economy that has been growing faster than its overall (not urban) population since at least 1997, and it is an increasingly productive par-
ticipant in international trade flows. In 1983 the total value of its exports and
imports combined was approximately $36 million. In 2003 the combined
total of exports and imports was almost 10 times as large.[52] South Africa's
economy has also been growing faster than its population at least since 1997,
but its exports and imports have only doubled since 1983.[53] Per capita gross

domestic product statistics for 2003 reflect the extent of poverty in many fevered crescent countries relative to Mexico and South Africa.[54]

The populations of Egypt, Indonesia even before the tsunami of 2004 (post-tsunami averages will be even lower), India, Pakistan, Bangladesh, and even oil-"rich" Nigeria were considerably less well off than the populations of Mexico and South Africa. The level of Pakistan's exports and imports has remained virtually unchanged since 1993 (statistics are not available for earlier periods). At a time when worldwide trade had mushroomed, Pakistan's exports in 1993 were approximately $17 billion and by 2003 had only grown to $21 billion.[55] Egypt has experienced approximately the same level of increase as Pakistan.[56] Bangladesh's imports and exports have more than doubled since 1993, but the increase was from an exceptionally low base of only $6 billion.[57]

Poverty is, of course, a problem in and of itself. It is also a reflection of the carrying capacity of the domestic economy to compensate for the failings and incapacities of government, particularly with respect to major urban population centers. Thus it is fair to conclude that the private sector in many of the fevered crescent states will be less capable than the private sector in Mexico and South Africa of providing alternatives to the inadequate public sector services.

The crime and domestic instability that is too often typical of cities that grow too fast exacerbates the problem of economic growth. It hardly needs explication that foreign and domestic investors regard civil disorder and high levels of crime as strong disincentives to investment. Worse, violence causes disinvestment—a net reduction in the amount of capital available in an economy as domestic and international investors shift funds to less volatile locations. One study documented 146 major disturbances in cities of developing countries over the 1976–1992 period and concluded that the result of the disturbances was damage to badly needed infrastructure. The study also observed that such violence is most likely when the population expands beyond the capacity of municipal law enforcement mechanisms.[58] In other words, urban violence is most likely to occur in the types of cities we are examining, and this same violence exacerbates some of the conditions that made violence likely in the first place.

Nonetheless, the possibility of reverse quarantine on such difficult locales cannot be allowed for practical reasons. Increased interaction, contact, and eventually increased interdependence with such places will be almost inevitable.

Table 3.1 Per capita gross domestic product statistics for 2003

South Africa	$10,700
Mexico	$9,000
Egypt	$4,000
Indonesia	$3,200
Pakistan	$2,100
Bangladesh	$1,900
Nigeria	$900

Source: Central Intelligence Agency, *World Factbook 2004*, at
www.cia.gov/cia/publications/factbook/rankorder/2004rank.html.

Yet, while recent American administrations have been reluctant to fund even peacekeeping contingency funds in such regions, there has arisen a "bottom-up" response that suggests that such inaction is no longer tenable. Most notably, the Genocide Intervention Network is a private fund-raising initiative to provide funds for African Union troops to have the resources and material to intervene at the time and place of choosing—and not at the whim of the West.[59]

Evidence suggests, moreover, that many of the locales considered in this chapter are ripe for infiltration by external terrorists or for the growth of domestic terrorist organizations. In Nigeria, for example, the last two decades have witnessed a two-thirds decline in GDP, giving rise to unprecedented levels of poverty. Migration and land pressures have added to the mix. From 1999 to 2003, over 10,000 died as a result of violence springing from these declining conditions. Yet not all this violence is intrinsically enmeshed in political or religiously motivated violence. As former ambassador Princeton Lyman emphasized in congressional testimony, attacks in Nigeria are often concentrated against American interests in the oil industry. At the same time, the United States has no diplomatic presence in the Muslim-dominated north as well as no presence in the oil rich, though troubled, delta region of the country.[60]

While there are some initiatives that seek to further integrate these regions—particularly remote regions—into closer attention, more could be done. One promising program is the Pan Sahel Initiative, organized by the U.S. European Command, in conjunction with the Sahara-bordering desert states of Mauritania, Mali, Niger, Chad, Morocco, Algeria, and Tunisia, helping to assist in tracking movements of people, striking at terrorism, monitoring borders, and aiding further regional cooperation.[61]

The most dangerous precedent, however, is to funnel resources from one source of crisis (or crisis region) to another. Certainly, in the case of the fevered crescent, these emerging dangers are real, persistent, and growing. One of the less than promising indicators that this precedent of reallocating resources—"robbing Peter to pay Paul"—arose when the American embassy in Baghdad began staffing in 2004, personnel slots were taken (not created) from other embassies all over the world, including Nigeria.[62]

Such actions indicate something far less than strategic vision in action. For positive change to take place, more attention—not less—is necessary to address human issues, to seriously stem the rise and spread of terrorism, and to foster and engage new relationships that may become increasingly critical in the not distant future.

4

Rethinking Security

Although security is frequently considered in the analysis of international relations and strategy, military history, and national policy decisions, its essential meaning might better be widely debated than agreed on.[1] Commonly considered a basic concept in policy and academic debates, security at the national and subnational levels is an ephemeral quantity, and its definition is in large measure a reflection of the perspectives and physical situations of the student and analyst. Thus professors and analysts raised in a particular school—the realist school that emphasizes power relationships between states being the most influential at least in government circles—tend to interpret events with the blinders that the school's focus provided. The fact that realism has stood the test of time accounts for the skepticism that statesmen and many scholars have toward newer, wider definitions that would include many of the issues we have raised in this book. While we are partially sympathetic to realist concerns that broad definitions lead to prescriptions for the misuse of military power, or to the underestimation of the role that military forces should and must play in world affairs, we also recognize that many of the "security" issues we consider here do not—and cannot—fit within a state-centric, power-driven level of analysis.

There is, indeed, no denying that there is a hazard in adding the term *security* to either environmental or human-centered concerns. That hazard is analytical imprecision and its practical consequences: using the wrong tools for the right missions and forsaking the opportunity to establish focused institutions that are designed, unlike the military, for the purpose of addressing what are essentially nonmilitary concerns.

Another facet is that the definition of security must accommodate the fact that in the emerging urban landscape, the most important issues include not just "threats" but also vulnerabilities. Vulnerabilities are passive and may be long term. As we have attempted to illustrate, for example, population trends are creating both vulnerabilities and threats that must be addressed. The manifold challenges posed by rapid urbanization in the weak states of the Greater Near East and in other regions of the world make people more susceptible to physical and financial injury. The right definition of security should allow that every security issue does not need to be directly linked to the reality or immediate threat of physical violence by weapons-bearing people.

Thus an important acknowledgment should emerge here: those who form policy and make critical decisions on behalf of states and people must, ever increasingly, focus on aspects of traditional "national security," in which military forces will likely continue to play a prominent role, as well as human security, in which "nontraditional" security issues predominate, and in which nonmilitary and perhaps entirely new approaches will take center stage. If such a premise proves true, and in a future where both "hard" and "soft" security will matter, those involved in policy decisions (and those affected by such decisions) will increasingly need to focus on aspects of both threats and vulnerabilities. There is a crucial need, then, to recognize the difference between these two categories.

Distinguishing Threats, Sensing Vulnerabilities

A threat is identifiable and is often immediate; thus it most often elicits a linear response. Military force, for example, has traditionally been designed and sized against threats: to defend a state against external aggression by a known and well-equipped adversary to protect what are understood to be vital national interests, and to enhance the physical security of the state and its population. Thus the size of the U.S. and USSR nuclear arsenals during the cold war were linearly related in the sense that their sizes reflected generally accepted assessments in each country of the other's hostility and military capability. The U.S. budget processes essentially mandated the identification of credible threat scenarios and attempts to keep the level of military investments in rough equivalence to the magnitude of the threat scenarios. In short, for government budgeting purposes a threat is generally acknowledged or clearly visible. Unenvisioned threats may, of course, develop but until they become visible, they do not factor into budgets or plans.

Vulnerabilities are less clear and less immediate. Often vulnerabilities are signaled by suggestive indicators linked to a complex interdependence among related issues and not always suggestive of a correct or even adequate response. While disease, hunger, unemployment, crime, social conflict, criminality, narco-trafficking, political repression, and environmental hazards impact security of states and individuals, the best response to these related issues is not at all clear. Canada, for example, has emphasized the relevance of human and environmental security to "high politics," but its decision to restructure its armed forces to attend to these issues bespeaks uncertainty about the likely consequences of that decision. Modifying existing institutions may be helpful, but the reality remains that the solution to most of these problems lies in the nonmilitary realm. Making the armed forces more like a nonmilitary entity may not be enough to solve the nontraditional problems, but will be enough to cause failure in addressing the traditional ones.

Unlike threats, vulnerabilities are not clearly perceived, often not well understood, and almost always a source of contention among conflicting views. Compounding the problem, the time element in the perception of vulnerability must be recognized. Some suggest that the core identity in a security response to issues involving human or environmental security is that of recognizing a condition of extreme vulnerability. Extreme vulnerability can arise from living under conditions of severe economic deprivation resulting from natural disasters, war, and internal conflicts. Thus long-term human development attempts might appear to make little or no sense and offer no direct help.

R. H. Tawney, describing rural China in 1931, noted the extreme vulnerability among peasants through a powerful image: "There are districts in which the position of the rural population is that of a man standing permanently up to the neck in the water, so that even a ripple is sufficient to drown him."[2] In such instances, the need for intervention is immediate, but as we know, the international community has tended to do little to prevent the ripples from forming or to rescue Tawney's figurative peasant. What hope then can there be for decisive action on the less urgent vulnerabilities that we have examined in this book? This is a real issue. In chapter 7, we offer suggestions for overcoming the international community's tendency to dismiss these long-term vulnerabilities as either too difficult or too distant.

Indeed, policy analysts and decision makers are most often driven by crisis response rather than the needs of long-term strategic planning. Given the uncertainty, the complexity, and the sheer nonlinear unpredictability of the long-term vulnerabilities that are creeping up on us, the typical response of the typical decision maker is to respond by doing nothing at all. The more appropriate response is to take an adaptive posture, to avoid the impulse to act purely on gut instinct, and to recognize what variables, indicators, and analogies from past examples might best inform the basis of action.[3]

To be clear: avoiding disastrous long-term impacts of creeping vulnerabilities such as the ones that are being generated by fast urban growth in weak states requires strategic planning and investment. To date, states and international institutions seem woefully unprepared for such strategic necessities. Moreover, environmental and human security, since they are contentious issues, often fall victim to the do nothing response because of their vulnerability-based conditions in which the causes are not clearly identifiable and are subject to debate. Another fact may be that political leaders have less confidence in the tools for remediation than in the traditional tools of military force and diplomacy at the state level, in particular military cooperation and diplomacy among in-the-light states.

There is a saying that if all you have is a hammer, every problem begins to look like a nail. It might perhaps be more apt to say that when one has only a hammer, the problems that do not look like nails are ignored. An obvious solution would be to add new tools to the repertoire and thus equip ourselves to do something about the problems that are not nails.

Unfortunately, the obvious solution is one that governments have been reluctant to choose because it would involve reallocating funds from existing programs with vested interests. Another reason might be the intuition that once these new tools are acquired, the result would be engagement in messy long-term projects that are not politically popular and, moreover, do not yield results that can be meaningfully measured on a quarterly or even an annual basis. In democracies, the ability to demonstrate results for overseas expenditures (domestic expenditures have stronger vested interests and are regarded less skeptically by the public) is crucial to the political success of the leaders responsible for the expenditures and for the continued funding of the overseas programs.

These emerging vulnerabilities will not mitigate or replace more traditional hard security dilemmas. Rather, we will see the continued reality of threat-based conditions contend with the rise of various vulnerability-based urgencies. By their very nature, creeping vulnerabilities will likely receive the least attention, even as their interdependent complexities grow increasingly difficult to address over time. Admittedly, suppositions here that insist on a distinction between threat and vulnerability become somewhat suspect in the so-called Age of Terror. While no one doubts that certain states and actors are under threat from al-Qaeda and other terrorist groups, the shadowy nature of such loosely grouped networks defies the traditional sense of threat. Loose terrorist networks often display the following characteristics: the capacity to operate "in the dark" so that their size, strategy toward a particular state, and readiness to act in a particular state are not as visible as traditional threats; the ability to operate effectively as a lateral and regional network in many locations at once; and the ability to learn, self-organize, and reconstitute more quickly than states after experiencing a setback.[4] As such, these networks operate on the fault line between threat and vulnerability, and too narrow a focus on either threat or vulnerability will only lead to frustration—and failure.

Urbanization and Creeping Vulnerabilities

The difference between urbanization in the emerging world and in the so-called developed world, reviewed briefly in the first chapter, reminds us that the center of gravity of the vulnerabilities and threats associated with urbanization is in the Lagos-Cairo-Karachi-Jakarta arc. The vulnerabilities and threats that we have discussed in this book (for example, violence in and around overcrowded and undergoverned cities; diseases whose spread is facilitated by inadequate public health infrastructure in those cities and at the same time promoted by a vibrant international transportation network based in developed cities; isolated rural areas virtually conceded to criminal and terrorist organizations) are interconnected. Thus the bigger cities become, the bigger their impact will be on their political and natural environments, and the worse the natural environment becomes, the more difficult it will be for cities to meet the health, safety, and economic expectations of their residents.

An example of creeping vulnerability, one in which outcomes do not necessarily lead to violence but do lead to economic and environmental stress, can be found in the complex interrelationship between water use, agriculture, and the expectations of emerging societies and adapting lifestyles of the future. In 1900, 1.6 billion people populated the earth; in 2000, that number reached 6 billion. In most countries people are also living longer. In 1900, a male American had a life expectancy of 47 years; in 2000, that life expectancy reached 77 years. Given such statistics, one would assume that water consumption by individuals for drinking, cooking, and bathing might increase by a factor of 5 or 6. In reality, water consumption has exploded by a factor of 10—from 500 cubic meters per capita in 1900 to 5,000 in 2000. This indicates that only some of the growth in water consumption can be attributed to population growth per se.

The real "explosion" in water usage has resulted from the expansion of agriculture.[5] Indeed, agriculture accounts for 70 percent of all water use and accelerating demand for agricultural production is, of course, a direct function of urbanization. As cities expand, farms need to increase their output. The only way that they can increase output is by increasing the critical input: water.

By the early 1960s, virtually all available arable land was being exploited in one way or another. Since then, the world's population has doubled and incomes in many countries have jumped. This has caused the demand for grains to surge along with demand for other farm products. Production has kept pace with demand as various forms of agriculture have become more intensive, scientific, rationalized, and efficient. But a more productive agricultural sector comes at a price—greater water consumption.

Developed states are particularly heavy consumers of water, but all urban centers cause water consumption to rise. As an example of how an economically advanced state uses water resources, consider these linkages: 82 percent of American cropland is not cultivated for crops that will be consumed by humans. Rather, these crops are grown for other food products—refined and processed foods—or for livestock feed. Indeed, 80 percent of the grain produced in the United States is used to feed cattle, pigs, and chicken that are later butchered for human consumption. Much of the emerging world has started to follow America's example. In 1960, Mexico fed 5 percent of its grain to livestock; today 45 percent of Mexican grain is fed to animals. Roughly the same trends have been observed in other countries. For example, the percentages for Egypt went from 3 to 31 over the same period. China, with a sixth of the world's population, has gone from 8 to 26 percent.[6]

These developments and trends argue that it is time to rethink security. For all the talk in policy centers and the academy about new world orders, networks of international dependence, and the shrinking of the nation-state's power, the traditional definition of security has not been seriously challenged in the context of the trends that are going to shape the world in the next few decades. As we have noted, the single most important of those—in terms of the ramifications on security—is the rapid urbanization in what we call the fevered crescent.

What Do We Mean by "Security"?

In the classical sense, security—from the Latin *securitas*—refers to tranquility and freedom from care, or what Cicero termed the absence of anxiety upon which the fulfilled life depends. Numerous governmental and international reports that focus on "freedom from fear" and "freedom from want" emphasize a pluralist notion that security is a basic need.

Yet in the once widely accepted realist understanding, the state was the sole guarantor of this freedom. Without the order that the state created (or imposed, depending upon one's perspective), there would be violence at the local level and war at the regional level. In this view, security extended from the state down to individuals. The individual's security depended upon the state's security. Conversely, the stable state extended upward in its relations to influence the security of the overall international system. The overall system grew to promote security by supporting the stability of states. Individual security, stemming from the liberal thought of the Enlightenment, was also considered both a unique and collective good. Adam Smith, for example, in *The Theory of Moral Sentiments*, mentions only the security of the sovereign, who possesses a standing army to protect him against popular discontent and is thus "secure" and able to allow his subject the liberty of political "remonstrance." By contrast, M. J. de Condorcet's argument in the late eighteenth century suggested that the economic security of individuals was an essential condition for political society. Fear—and the fear of fear—were for Condorcet the enemies of liberal politics.[7]

Moreover, despite the abundance of theoretical and conceptual approaches in recent history, the right of states to protect themselves under the rubric of "national security" and through traditional instruments of power (political, economic, and especially military) has never been directly challenged. The responsibility, however, for the guarantee of the individual good—under any security rubric—has never been obvious.

It is significant that nontraditional security issues that have long plagued the so-called emerging world—issues that include environmental degradation, resource scarcity, transnational issues of criminality and terrorism—can increasingly affect the policy decisions and future choices for powerful states and world leaders as well. As disparate as these nontraditional issues may be, the developed world is now confronted with similar, human-centered vulnerabilities that had often been present previously only for developing regions. The implications of this changing security environment for the analyst and policy maker are profound.

The future may well require decision makers to focus on a broad—and broadening—understanding of the meaning of security. The 1994 United Nations Development Programme (UNDP) report, for example, attempted to recognize a conceptual shift that needed to take place:

> The concept of security has for too long been interpreted narrowly: as security of territory from external aggression, or as protection of national interests in foreign policy, or as global security from the threat of nuclear holocaust. It has been related to nation-states more than people. . . . Forgotten were the legitimate concerns of ordinary people who sought security in their daily lives. For many of them, security symbolized protection from the threat of disease, hunger, unemployment, crime [or terrorism], social conflict, political repression, and environmental hazards. With the dark shadows of the cold war receding, one can see that many conflicts are within nations rather than between nations.[8]

In 2003, the UN Commission on Human Security expanded this concept to include protection for peoples suffering through violent conflict inside states, for those who have been displaced from their homes by natural catastrophes or war, refugees who have fled their homelands to escape conflict or persecution, and for noncombatants in post-conflict situations who are struggling to repair the damage to their communities. The Commission even considered the concept of security to call for improving conditions of poverty, health, and knowledge.[9]

Undoubtedly, increasing numbers now speak out on behalf of what the International Commission on Intervention and State Sovereignty has termed the "responsibility to protect": the responsibility of some state or agency (whether it be a superpower such as the United States or an institution such as the United Nations) to enforce the principle of security that sovereign states owe to their citizens. It must be noted here that there is a dark side to the proposition that an entity outside a state (be it another state, a group of states, or the United Nations) has the responsibility to protect the security of individuals inside the state. A responsibility is meaningless without the right and the ability to act on behalf of the principles or peoples for which the responsibility exists. Thus the responsibility to protect something or someone must equate to the right to intervene. It has always been the case that the strong are better able than the weak to act on a responsibility such as this. In the topology of power, this means that dominant states will intervene at the time and place of their choosing, and there is always the risk that these interventions will serve their traditionally defined national interests even when the human security labels are used.

The Ethics of Security

It would be reasonable at this juncture to touch upon the ethics of security and its place in the actions of states and actors. According to H. Richard Niebuhr, a responsible ethic (which would encompass an ethics of intervention) embraces the Greek concept of *themis*, the law of the community that is based on the essential principle of justice. This ethic should be driven by a social process that is responsive and accountable to nothing less than an "international community."[10]

Admittedly, such a paradigm of responsible security ethics would prove difficult to implement, even if its governing principles were widely accepted. Yet it does seem appropriate to ask whether or not there is a need, or even a possibility, for establishing a framework for ethical security action, including when to intervene. While some have focused on establishing capabilities at the United Nations and/or in nongovernmental organizations such as Human Rights Watch to determine basic economic, social, and human needs, it might also be appropriate to consider whether or not it is possible to establish an ethical framework for security as Niebuhr advocated.[11] The driving force of responsible security ethics entails assessment of both the sovereignty of a state and the responsibility of external states to provide support for a state's continued survival while simultaneously protecting the people inside the state. The Iraq intervention in 2003, in principle at least, was partially based on the belief that social justice, participatory freedom, and economic development would help liberate the Iraqi, remove Saddam Hussein from power, and mitigate the proliferation of weapons of mass destruction.[12] Even as Kyle Grayson emphatically stresses that treating (specifically human) security policy as an *ethos*—indeed even a critical transformative ethos—is essential, it remains unclear why an ethos of national security, in principle, should be by any means markedly different than the practice of human security, even one based on reciprocity.[13]

While Reinhold Niebuhr believed that disparities between states were inevitable and that states, like human beings, have an innate desire to dominate others, even Niebuhr assented to the idea that "the goal of modern man must be a society in which there will be enough justice, and in which coercion will be sufficiently nonviolent to prevent his common enterprise from issuing into common disaster."[14] John Rawls adequately defined this "well-ordered society" in the broadest sense as "one designed to advance the good of its members and effectively regulated by a public conception of justice." Equally, Rawls emphasized the plurality of support for the common acceptance of the principles of justice and the essential requirement for institutions that satisfy these principles.[15] This ideal, as Timothy Garton Ash notes, is also the essential complex tension between intellectual or emotional acceptance of the principles qua principles and the difficulties associated with action based upon those principles that characterized twentieth-century Europe and will characterize the future order.[16] The most dramatic examples of the tension between an accepted principle and action consistent with the principle are the 1994 genocide in Rwanda and the more recent mass killings in the Darfur region of Sudan. No one rejected the principles in the international convention on genocide—other than the principle that the international community would take timely decisive action to prevent it, rather than responding after hundreds of thousands had been killed.

Paradoxically, moves toward resolution of human security dilemmas often occur only after the application of military force by a major power, regional rival states, or parties within the affected state. Without action now, this may be the sequence as well with respect to the emerging environmental and human security problems in the fevered crescent. It may be that human security problems will not be seriously addressed at all except in the aftermath of war as for example has been the case in Iraq and Afghanistan. Obviously the better course is to begin addressing them now—in a non-military (rather than premilitary) context. Thus there is a true need to allow alternative perspectives to broaden our thinking.

Those who emphasize military security, especially American analysts and policy makers, at the expense of other security issues will find that they are leading themselves into the paradoxical but ironically self-fulfilling situation: the more one seeks to avoid addressing nontraditional security issues, the more one may be driven to militarily intervene in the future. As the interventions in Somalia, the Balkans, Afghanistan, and Iraq illustrate, traditionally narrow definitions of national security and traditional applications of military force are not enough. The ultimate success or failure of these actions will not be clear for many years, and whatever military successes in the field there have been, their effects could very well be unraveled by inattention in the immediate future to the broader range of security issues.

Although it is unclear how permanent or deep the damage was from the 2003 U.S.–European transatlantic rift over intervention in Iraq, there are warning signals that strongly indicate to us that an international ethic of intervention will not be achieved soon. As Robert Kagan notes, a crisis of legitimacy has emerged since September 11:

> The fact remains that the Kosovo war was illegal, and not only because it lacked Security Council authorization: Serbia had not committed any aggression against another state but was slaughtering its own ethnic Albanian population. The intervention therefore violated the sovereign equality of all nations, a cardinal principle—of the UN Charter and the bedrock principle of international law for centuries. During the Kosovo conflict, Henry Kissinger warned that "the abrupt abandonment of the concept of national sovereignty" risked unmooring the world from any notion of order, legal or otherwise. Many Europeans rejected this complaint at the time. Back then . . . before the Iraq war . . . they did not seem to believe that international legitimacy resided exclusively with the Security Council, or in the UN Charter, or even in traditional principles of international law. Instead they believed in the legitimacy of their common post-modern moral values.[17]

In 2003, during the dispute over Iraq, those postmodern values did not seem to be universally shared or even understood, and many European states insisted upon Security Council authorization—the very principle they dismissed over Kosovo. Whichever view of Security Council authorization holds sway in Paris and Berlin in the future, it is clear that when major powers, primarily the United States, forego international support for the sake of national interests, the rift will not soon heal.

Shrinking the Gap

All of these troubling outcomes are only exacerbated in the agony of those who are pushed aside, annihilated, or remain fortunate enough to flee (with nothing). In redrawing the map of the future, the focus again must shift to asking: What are the long-term consequences of failing to recognize creeping vulnerabilities? While it may at first seem a stretch, for example, it is nevertheless pertinent to recall that the protection of displaced Arabs in refugee camps following the 1967 Arab-Israeli war led eventually to the *intifadas* of the last 20 years.[18] The displacement of Hutus and Tutsis from the 1994 genocide in Rwanda is directly related to the violent conflicts that swept through the Democratic Republic of Congo, where reasonable estimates place the death toll from various conflicts in excess of 3.5 million since 1997. Indeed, a future Balkan conflict may now be taking root in the weak economic conditions, corrupt political institutions, and bands of angry young men with nowhere to go and nothing to look forward to in the streets and ruined foundations of Kosovo, Bosnia, and Serbia.

Thus, in considering whether such frameworks might be viable for the future, it is important to step away from applying such a template only to crisis response or the extreme vulnerability of Tawney's drowning peasant. Arguably, the seeds of disaster in Bosnia-Herzegovina and Kosovo did not begin in 1998; rather, they began in the aftermath of the Second World War and flared up, again and again, during the 1980s—as illustrations of creeping vulnerability that were repeatedly ignored. Yet the consequence and the cost to the international community of not investing in the Balkans in the right way and early enough could be at least 50 years of political and military engagement—and economic assistance. In comparison, the reconstruction of Iraq remains a far more daunting task.

Although it seems attractive to insist on exclusionary concepts that insist on desecuritization, privileged referent objects, and the "belief" that threats and vulnerabilities are little more than social constructions, all these concepts work in theory but fail in practice.[19] While it is true that traditional and national security paradigms can, and likely will continue to, dominate issues that involve human security vulnerabilities—and even in some instances mistakenly confuse vulnerabilities as threats—there are distinct linkages between these security concepts and applications. With regard to environmental security, for example, Norman Myers recognized these linkages decades ago: "National security is not just about fighting forces and weaponry. It relates to watersheds, croplands, forests, genetic resources, climate, and other factors that rarely figure in the minds of military experts and political leaders, but increasingly deserve, in their collectivity, to rank alongside military approaches as crucial in a nation's security."[20]

Ultimately, though, we are far from what O'Hanlon and Singer term a global intervention capability on behalf of "humanitarian transformation."[21] Granted, we now have the threat of mass casualty terrorism anytime, anywhere—and states and regions are responding differently to this challenge. Yet the global community today also continues to face many of the same problems of the 1990s: civil wars, faltering states, humanitarian crises. We are no closer to addressing how best to solve these challenges, even as they impact issues of environmental, human, and national security.

Yet the creation of a sense of urgency to act—even on some issues that may not have impact for years or even decades to come—is perhaps the only appropriate first response. The real cost of not investing, in the right way and early enough, in the places where trends and effects are accelerating in the wrong direction is likely to be decades and decades of economic and political frustration and, potentially, military engagement. Rather than justifying intervention (especially military), we ought to be justifying investment, and we should start recognizing the strategic value of investment to our own security.

Simply acknowledging the immensities of these challenges is obviously not enough. Radical improvements in public infrastructure and support for better governance, particularly in states and municipalities along the Lagos-Cairo-Karachi-Jakarta arc, will improve security and create the conditions for shrinking the gap between expectations and opportunity.

Recent history suggests that military intervention as the first line of response to human security conditions underscores a seriously flawed approach. Moreover, those who advocate that a state's disconnectedness from globalization is inversely proportional to the likelihood of military (read, U.S.) intervention fail to recognize unfolding realities.[22] Both middle-power and major-power states as well as the international community must increasingly focus on long-term creeping vulnerabilities in order to avoid crises response to conditions of extreme vulnerability. Admittedly, some human security proponents have recently soured on the viability of the concept in the face of recent "either with us or against us" power politics.[23] At the same time, and in a bit more positive light, some have clearly recognized the sheer impossibility of international power politics continuing to feign indifference in the face of moral categories. As J. Peter Burgess notes, "For all its evils, one of the promises of globalization is the unmasking of the intertwined nature of ethics and politics in the complex landscape of social, economic, political, and environmental security."[24]

While it is still not feasible to establish a threshold definition for security that neatly fits all concerns and arguments, it would be a tragic mistake to assume that national, human, and environmental security—both as concepts and as bases for policy decisions—are mutually harmonious rather than more often locked in conflict with each other. Aspects of security resident in each concept are indeed themselves embedded with extraordinary contradictions. Human security, in particular, is not now, nor should likely ever be, the mirror image of national security.

Yet these contradictions are not the crucial recognition here. To the contrary, rather than focusing on the security issues themselves, we should be focusing on the best multidimensional approaches to confronting and solving them. One approach, which might avoid the massive tidal impact of creeping vulnerabilities, is to sharply make a rudder shift from constant crisis intervention toward strategic planning, strategic investment, and strategic attention. Clearly, the time is now to reorder our entire approach to how we address—or fail to address—security.

Governance and Democracy

"I should regard it as a great misfortune for mankind if liberty were to exist all over the world under the same features."

Alexis de Tocqueville, *Democracy in America*

There are many reasons why states in the fevered crescent will experience (and, indeed, some are already experiencing) substantial difficulties in governing—providing effective public services to—their exploding urban populations and at the same time keeping control of distant, inaccessible, and underpopulated rural areas. In this chapter we will explore those factors and consider how they might affect their approaches to effective and democratic forms of government. It should be noted that we accept the principle that democracy is not merely the wave of the present; it is very likely a sine qua non for effective governance in the future. Democracy can take many forms—or rather there are many forms of democracy that can build the trust and confidence that should exist between a citizenry and its government. What is important is not the form but the function of enabling the people to have a meaningful voice in the government's policy-making process. Therefore, the specific forms of the United States and the United Kingdom, to name the most aggressive promoters of democracy around the world, may not be completely suitable to the states of the fevered crescent or for that matter to transitioning states in other parts of the world.

Further, much of what is often included in discussions of the benefits of democracy are not, in fact, direct benefits of democracy at all but are instead functions of power-balancing that were designed to reduce the power of the state as a whole or of particular branches of the state apparatus. The obvious example is the system of checks and balances in the U.S. government. Another important benefit that is often incorrectly attributed to democratic governance is "rule of law," ultimately a legal system that is stable enough to give citizens confidence in the predictability of their interactions with each other and with the government.

The most important reasons why states in the fevered crescent will struggle with the challenges posed by massive-scale urbanization revolve around timing. Not only did the urbanization trend crest relatively quickly but the

Table 5.1 Independence day

Country	Independence attained
Nigeria	1960
Egypt	1952 (when British troops withdrew)
India	1947
Pakistan	1947
Bangladesh	1971 (formerly East Pakistan)
Indonesia	1949

crest arose while the states were still relatively new. Indeed, most of the states in the fevered crescent are little more than a half century old. Most became fully independent only after World War II, and many have experienced war and/or civil war during their first 50 years of existence. Table 5.1 shows some examples.

As is typical of many newly formed states, these states have spent a considerable amount of energy and resources dealing with territorial disputes with neighboring states and/or with internal separatist movements. Unlike most of the other states in table 5.1, Nigeria has not been involved in a major interstate war, but throughout its history it has had a number of coups and minor rebellions. This is not surprising given that Nigeria contains 250 ethnic groups.[1] There was also a major civil war in the late 1960s over the attempted secession of the state of Biafra, which was eventually and forcefully reintegrated into the state. Egypt has fought four wars with Israel, three of which inflicted serious damage on the country. The 1967 war resulted in the loss of a substantial amount of Egyptian territory (Sinai, which was in Israeli hands from 1967 to 1979). Egypt also participated in the civil war in Yemen. As many as 80,000 Egyptian troops were engaged in the Yemeni civil war during the early to mid-1960s.[2] Pakistan fought wars with India in 1947–1948 and 1965 and experienced a civil war in 1971 that resulted in the dismemberment of the country. Pakistan's archrival, India, intervened in the civil war on behalf of the Bengali separatist movement, and at war's end the Bengali provinces, which had constituted East Pakistan, became the independent state of Bangladesh. Like Nigeria, Indonesia's conflicts have been largely internal as it has had to deal with a major communist insurgency in the 1960s and various separatist movements in East Timor (now independent of Indonesia), Papua (seized from the Dutch in 1962), and Aceh (devastated by the 2004 tsunami).

The perhaps unavoidable consequence of this military activity has been that the national governments have focused on external threats and internal separatism at the expense of attention to building the infrastructure of economic development and the delivery of public services. Poor to begin with, the new states were compelled (or chose to compel themselves) to overinvest in military infrastructure and underinvest in other forms of infrastructure. Thus the relative youth of the modern fevered crescent states in combination with their security-related "growing pains" is one reason why they are ill-equipped to meet the challenge of massive urbanization.

A second reason for the complex difficulties that emerge in the fevered crescent is the speed at which the urbanization has occurred. By 2015 Lagos will have grown more than twentyfold since Nigeria achieved independence. Karachi will also have grown about twentyfold since Pakistan's independence. Jakarta and Cairo will have grown ninefold and sevenfold respectively by 2015.[3] Even the growth rates such as those of Cairo and Jakarta are high relative to the growth rates in other, more successful cities over equivalent blocks of time. The population of the city of Los Angeles, for example, multiplied "only" about fivefold during the 50-year period of its fastest growth, 1920–1970. Tokyo's population grew at an even slower pace than Los Angeles during the 1950–2000 time frame. Buenos Aires grew less than one and a half times, and the population of Rome did not even double between 1950 and 2000.[4]

Los Angeles warrants a closer look because it is not an old city in the same sense that historic national capitals like Cairo and Rome are and its growth spurt was from a low base, much like the newer capitals of Lagos and Dhaka, Bangladesh. In 1920, Los Angeles boasted a population of slightly less than 600,000. By 1970 the city's population was about 2.8 million.[5] It is important to note that this period of rapid urbanization took place long after the United States had become a nation and after California had become a state. California joined the United States in 1850, and the nation that California joined was itself already 70 years old at the time and had developed a substantial economy with established national infrastructures. By the time Los Angeles started to grow, the state of California itself had already experienced considerable economic growth, and the state and national infrastructures and economies complemented and supported the municipal structures in Los Angeles.

This means that the city of Los Angeles had important advantages during its growth spurt that were not available to many of the emerging megacities in the fevered crescent and will not be available to them in the future. Specifically, Los Angeles' population growth was not coincident with the formative years of its parent nation or even of its parent state. As a city, Los Angeles was better able to provide public services to its burgeoning population during the five decades of its fastest growth than Lagos, Karachi, and

Jakarta were during the past 50 years. Cities such as Lagos, Karachi, Jakarta, and to a lesser extent Cairo not only faced much more dramatic growth rates than Los Angeles did but their growth spurt occurred before their national government had developed effective sinews of national government, other than in the military sphere. Moreover, those governmental sinews will not have developed sufficiently in the next several decades to accommodate the next growth spurts—unless the international community bands together to help.

Further, the growth of the population of Los Angeles and, for that matter, other cities in North America and Western Europe took place after the national identities had solidified and there were no major political fault lines between regions or religious groups. (Racial tensions existed in the United States, of course, but they did not seriously challenge the governmental structure.) The same cannot be said for some of the new countries in the fevered crescent where significant regional, ethnic, and religious divisions continue to exist. For example, there are still substantial internal pressures to readjust the constitutional structure of the Nigerian government to accommodate some of the country's 250 ethnic groups or to balance the constitutional expectations of Muslims and non-Muslims with respect to the relationship between the government and Islamic religious law—as evidenced by a "National Political Reform Conference" that convened in 2005 to debate basic structure-of-government issues such as the relationship of regions to the central government.[6]

Other Reasons beyond Timing

There are other, more contemporary reasons why governance and public services in cities such as Lagos, Cairo, Karachi, and Jakarta have failed to keep pace with population growth. These same reasons will also compromise the capabilities of tomorrow's cities in the fevered crescent. One is the general poverty of the states and the populations involved. Per capita incomes in many countries in these regions of the world are extremely low. Moreover, the individuals who move from the countryside into the city or who are born in underserved shantytowns inside the city generally have low levels of education and contribute relatively little to the growth of the municipal economy or to the revenue base of the municipal government.

Another reason is that urbanization in the future will occur in the context of a radically restructured technological and economic world order. With respect to technological change, one of the most important involves communications. The widespread availability of broadcast media, personal communications devices, and access to the Internet are bound to have a dramatic impact on the process of urbanization—if only by heightening the expectations that city dwellers have of their government and their awareness of its failings relative to other urban entities.

Stalin reputedly believed that one of the main purposes of censorship was to prevent dissatisfied or disgruntled individuals from drawing support from each other. His theory evidently was that if criticisms of the Soviet regime were allowed to air, potential opponents of the regime would recognize that they were not alone and this recognition would embolden them to express additional criticisms. What was to Stalin a vicious cycle of greater criticism would thus potentially form and eventually meld into political opposition. The ubiquity of print and broadcast media and the Internet as well as the falling prices of telecommunication equipment mean that as a practical matter, municipal and national governments in the Lagos-Cairo-Karachi-Jakarta arc will find it impossible to do what Stalin attempted: to prevent information that would raise expectations or reinforce dissatisfaction from becoming widely available to the public. This will unquestionably lead to pressure on the governments to improve public services. It may also lead to urban disorder if and when the services are not improved. As noted earlier, urban disorder tends to only make the situation worse if it results in damage to infrastructure and causes disinvestment or deters new private investment.

Changes in the economic world order are also factors that may exert a deleterious effect on Nigeria, Egypt, Pakistan, Indonesia, and the other states along the fevered crescent. Economic globalization means that there are no longer any significant protected markets—except, of course, for the respective domestic markets of countries determined to pursue the self-defeating policy of autarchy or wholesale import substitution. These policies are self-defeating in the long term because the domestic markets at least in states that we are focusing on are generally too poor to support vibrant or even modern industries. Their domestic markets have already demonstrated the inability to provide jobs to a growing population. They have also been unable to generate government revenues substantial enough to support an expanded, more effective public service infrastructure or for the private sector to generate enough capital to compensate for the public sector shortfall. As we have noted earlier, the financial cost of building military capabilities—as justified as it may have been given the turbulence that these states have faced in their formative years—is a major contributor to the states' inability to fund domestic infrastructure.

The size of the investment that would be required to enable the emerging megacities to effectively manage their growth is daunting, and the international community of nations is not investing enough in helping improve municipal governance. Development aid or "official development assistance" (essentially foreign aid that is not designed to alleviate the immediate consequences of a natural disaster such as a famine or flood, or to minister to the victims of civil war) has not kept pace with the need. In fact, during the 1990s, the level of global development assistance actually declined slightly in terms of real value. It rose between 2003 and 2005 due largely to sharp increases in aid to postwar Afghanistan and Iraq and in 2005 and 2006 to Indonesia for reconstruction after the December 2004 tsunami.[7] In other words, development aid is not at high enough levels to meet the challenges of tomorrow, and the increases in recent years have been targeted at unique situations and do not address the issues of megacity infrastructure and governance.

Indeed, development aid goes to a variety of programs and projects, many of which have little to do with the problems of mushrooming cities. For example, the United Nations established eight "millennium development goals" in 2000: eradicate extreme poverty and hunger; achieve universal primary education; promote gender equality and empower women; reduce child mortality; improve maternal health; combat HIV/AIDS, malaria, and other diseases; ensure environmental stability; and develop a global partnership for development.[8]

Each of these goals is extremely worthwhile, but collectively they do not do enough to directly address the challenge of building governance infrastructures, and much depends upon how the United Nations meets the goals. For example, if eradicating hunger is accomplished through traditional feeding programs and technical assistance to farmers, then the cities and their private sectors will not be in any better position to manage food distribution programs after the UN programs wind down. Promoting gender equity is an important objective that is certainly consistent with democratic principles, but empowering women may only have a very indirect and delayed effect on the capacity of the city to deliver public services. Moreover, as the United States has found in Afghanistan and Iraq (and as the UN and nongovernmental organizations have also found in Sudan and other places), promotion of social values such as gender equity can actually set back reform by increasing resistance to all forms of change.

The United Nations estimates that achieving the Millennium Development Goals will require investment of about $100 billion annually in addition to the mobilization of domestic resources. However, development assistance is only about 70 percent of that figure and, as noted above, the figure is inflated by short-term priorities in Iraq, Afghanistan, and exurban provinces of Indonesia.[9]

There is, indeed, a vicious circle with respect to the kinds of reforms and capability building that will be required in the cities of the fevered crescent. To a significant extent, investing in improvements to the public services infrastructure does not result in immediate improvements in the services themselves or in the health and well-being of the individuals and families that constitute the demand for the public services. For example, building a school will require a year or more of planning and effort, but it will be many years before that school graduates students and perhaps another few years before the graduated students begin to make a difference in the local economy. Similarly, building a police station and recruiting police officers does not have an immediate effect on public safety. The officers have to be trained and then establish their presence in crime-ridden neighborhoods before the crime rates in those neighborhoods are affected.

As a result, there is an understandable tendency to invest development assistance funds in projects that make an immediate difference, rather than projects whose direct outcome is deferred and whose impact is, further-more, harder to evaluate than projects in which progress can be measured by counting the numbers of individuals that are fed or inoculated against a contagious disease. This is, of course, analogous to the choice that govern-mental and private donors make between investing in development assis-tance or disaster relief, and the trend in recent years has been for donors to increase relief rather than development assistance.

Another aspect of the vicious circle facing the new megacities is that pri-vate investment is necessary for the economies of the new megacities to flourish, but private investors will generally invest elsewhere until such time as the municipalities have demonstrated that they have already mastered the challenges of maintaining infrastructure and delivering public service. One aspect of globalization is that there are more markets than ever before to which capital can flow freely. As a result investors have many choices about where to invest, and unmanaged cities are not likely to be among the preferred locations. Since there are large numbers of poor people and un-derserved neighborhoods in the better-governed cities of China and India, investments in these cities will contribute to the UN millennium develop-ment goals but will do nothing to address the broadly defined security issues of the feral city.

Is Democracy the Solution?

According to the U.S. government, democracy provides the path to improved governance, and the only alternatives (fascism, communism, Islamism) to this view have largely been discredited. Of the three alternatives, Islamism with its emphasis on religious law and rule by religious leaders currently exerts the most influence in the fevered crescent.

In the September 2002 National Security Strategy document issued by the White House, democracy is touted as the only sustainable model for national success, and democracy promotion is said to "help make the world not just safer but better." Democracy has not always been assumed to be the only model for successful government—indeed, in 1968 Samuel P. Huntington wrote that the most important political distinction between countries was not the type but the degree of government:

> The differences between democracy and dictatorship are less than the differences between those countries whose politics embodies consensus, community legitimacy, organization, effectiveness, [and] stability, and those countries whose politics is deficient in these qualities.[10]

Thus any state that was well organized and whose government was perceived as both legitimate and acting in consonance with the consensus of its citizens with regard to the major directions of government policy was likely to be successful whether or not it met the criteria of being democratic. As we have sought to point out, many of the states in the Lagos-Cairo- Karachi-Jakarta arc are already deficient in these qualities and risk becoming more so as their urban populations burgeon. Robert D. Kaplan and the State Failure Task Force set up by the Clinton administration have seconded Huntington's implication that democratization and liberalization do not always lead to positive outcomes.[11]

How effective, therefore, will democracy promotion be in the world's unstable regions and particularly in the states with the world's most unstable cities? The question we seek to answer here is whether democracy—specifically American-style democracy—is, indeed, the best solution. One of the difficulties in answering this question is that American strategists and policy makers have been somewhat vague in explaining exactly what they mean by "promoting democracy."

The first explicit post–cold war articulation of a U.S. foreign policy strategy of promoting democracy was contained in the Clinton administration's 1994 National Security Strategy document. Its preface stated that one of the administration's three central goals was "to promote democracy abroad" because "democratic states are less likely to threaten our interests and more likely to cooperate with the United States to meet security threats and promote free trade and sustainable development."[12] The 1994 Strategy's premise was that democratic states by their very nature do not threaten the national interests of the United States, although the term *democracy* is not precisely defined. The next year's Strategy clarified that the objective was to increase the number of "democratic and free market nations" and "market democracies."[13] In the 1997, 1998, and 1999 Strategies—all issued by the Clinton administration—the objective was to "strengthen democratic and free market institutions and norms," with human rights highlighted as one of these norms. The 1999 Strategy emphasized democracy as an antidote to corruption.[14]

The Bush administration's September 2002 Strategy used even more ambitious and expansive wording in making similar claims about the desirability of promoting democracy, free markets, and human rights.

> The great struggles of the twentieth century between liberty and totalitarianism ended with a decisive victory for the forces of freedom—and a single sustainable model for national success: freedom, democracy, and free enterprise. In the twenty-first century, only nations that share a commitment to protecting basic human rights and guaranteeing political and economic freedom will be able to unleash the potential of their people and assure their future prosperity. People everywhere want to be able to speak freely; choose who will govern them; worship as they please; educate their children—male and female; own property; and enjoy the benefits of their labor. These values of freedom are right and true for every person, in every society—and the duty of protecting these values against their enemies is the common calling of freedom-loving people across the globe and across the ages. We will speak out honestly about violations of the nonnegotiable demands of human dignity using our voice and vote in international institutions to advance freedom; use our foreign aid to promote freedom and support those who struggle nonviolently for it, ensuring that nations moving toward democracy are rewarded for the steps they take; make freedom and the development of democratic institutions key themes in our bilateral relations, seeking solidarity and cooperation from other democracies while we press governments that deny human rights to move toward a better future; and take special efforts to promote freedom of religion and conscience and defend it from encroachment by repressive governments.[15]

It would seem, then, that when Washington has talked over the past several decades about promoting democracy, it has had in mind a set of governmental attributes that constitute a framework for a one-size-fits-all plan to propagate American-style democracies throughout the Greater Near East and the entire fevered crescent. But the experience in Afghanistan would suggest that one size cannot fit all and that Washington recognizes that fact even without admitting its full implications. For example, the highly touted elections to the 2002 Afghan Grand Council reflected practices that were inconsistent with the American model, including a quota system that ensured the participation of at least 150 women and a two-stage electoral process in which the 20 people with the highest number of votes in a district decided among themselves which one of them would represent the district. Although the Afghan experience was welcomed in Washington as a healthy step in the right direction, the White House's policy statements confirm that it prefers the largely fixed rule-set itemized in the Strategy (elections, universal suffrage, checks and balances/division of power, open and transparent government, freedom of the press, rule of law, free markets, freedom of worship, and freedom of speech). The greater number of these elements that a state exhibits with fidelity, the more secure, stable, and successful Washington believes it will be.

Apart from the specific impacts of each of these elements, there is assumed to be a collective—but hard to measure—value in their achievement that is directly beneficial to American national interests. As states become more democratic, it is thought that they will begin to share American values, including its foreign policy values. This, in turn, should increase the number of states willing to cooperate with the U.S. government on security matters as traditionally defined.

John Ikenberry, perhaps the leading advocate of the liberal analytical perspective, has argued that American statesmen from Woodrow Wilson to Bill Clinton and George W. Bush have, in one way or another, accepted the need for a community of shared values among states, particularly in the North American–Western European zones.[16] Obviously, such a community of shared values does not exist in some parts of the world, and Ikenberry and others (some of them in the Bush administration) do not enumerate exactly what values should be shared, how fully they must be shared, and who in each country should share them. Further, one of the lessons of recent history that Western statesmen (and some reformers in Egypt, Saudi Arabia, and elsewhere) have failed to learn is that the fevered crescent is not Europe. Numerous attempts have been made to transplant values from Europe to the Middle East, sub-Saharan Africa, and Southwest Asia. Democracy is not the first in this parade of exported values. Communism, national socialism, and fascism made substantial but temporary inroads in important states of the Greater Middle East during the 1970s and the years before World War II. It remains to be seen whether the region will be as resistant to democracy as it was to these other Western value systems.

Democracy May Become "Dangerous"

Shortly after the concept of state failure became a dominant theme in the 1990s, a literature emerged suggesting that, as a means of transitioning a society and region to stability, democracy can be dangerous—in the sense that it can introduce instability into precarious political situations and might result in violence or political chaos. Robert Kaplan's "The Coming Anarchy," which appeared in the February 1994 issue of the *Atlantic Monthly*, is a prime early example of this. Also of note in this regard is work begun by Thomas Homer-Dixon in the early 1990s at the University of Toronto's Peace and Conflict Studies Program that examines the linkages between environmental scarcity and conflict.

The work of the Central Intelligence Agency's State Failure Task Force was intended in part to be a response to the pessimistic assessments in Kaplan's "Coming Anarchy." Responding to the sense of increasing instability after the collapse of governance in many nations following the end of the cold war, the CIA claimed to have completed the first empirical and comprehensive effort to investigate the critical factors most responsible for state collapse and failure.[17]

Policy makers hoped this study of why certain states succeeded while others did not might provide indicators that could be used to obtain early warning of looming state failure in time for the international community to formulate suitable forms of preventive intervention. The Task Force's Phase II Mediated Environmental Model considered the predictive value of democratization, trade openness, environmental stress, material well-being, vulnerability, and capacity in state failure. Infant mortality, for example, because of its broader effect on other well-being issues, turned out to be one of the most accurate indicators of serious problems. The research found that partial democracies are particularly vulnerable and at elevated risk of state failure. That is to say, states undergoing the transition from an authoritarianism that suppressed societal tensions to a democracy that allowed these tensions to surface were putting themselves in a precarious situation.

In sub-Saharan Africa, partial democracies were found to be 11 times more likely to fail than autocratic states under similar conditions of environmental stress or population pressure, but it was also found that gradual transition to democracy would improve the state's long-term chances for success. The CIA Task Force members calculated that their model had a predictive accuracy of about 67 percent.[18] Critics of the Phase II model have cited this relatively low level of accuracy as a reason to doubt the model's predictive value. (After all, 67 percent equates to a grade of D and results in a high number of false positives.) With such a success rate, fully one-third of the warnings that would be generated for policy makers would be false alarms. John Steinbruner of the Center for International and Security Studies at Maryland thus argued:

> The single best statistical model to emerge from that exercise used three variables—openness to international trade, infant mortality, and democracy—to distinguish [roughly] 70 percent of the cases of state failure from the randomly chosen set two years in advance. The more open and more democratic countries with lower rates of infant mortality were less prone to violence. That result offers some insight, but it clearly is not refined enough to distinguish an imminent explosion from a chronic problem with the reliability that an effective policy of prevention would require. Were the same statistical performance to be achieved projecting forward rather than in retrospect—a feat not yet demonstrated—it would generate on average 50 false alarms a year (statistically expected episodes that do not occur) and would miss one actual event.[19]

Obviously a perfect state of predictive, or projective, modeling has yet to be attained. However, the data do suggest clearly that it is at the transition point to a democratic form of governance that a state's risk of failure and instability is greatest. Instability in any region ought to be of concern to the United States, but it is especially worrisome in the oil-rich and geostrategically important Greater Near East, Nigeria, and Indonesia. Thus, while democracy could enable security in the long term, the actual promotion of democracy in the near term might increase the immediate risk of instability.

The economy of a state undergoing democratic transition would also experience perturbations, as in Russia during the Yeltsin era. Economist Jeffrey Sachs observes that the transition phase challenges the state's economy and that the state will often require special short-term economic assistance from the international community.[20] The parallel to the Task Force findings is obvious. If it is not effectively managed, democracy promotion can result in severe disruption of the economic patterns within the state. The strain to the state's economic institutions only worsens the political instability.

There is another important potential side effect of democracy promotion: the assumption of power by anti-American, antiglobalization Islamists such as the recently ousted Taliban faction in Afghanistan.[21] While our focus in this book is on meeting the broad security challenges related to urban growth, rather than the challenge of overcoming obstacles to American foreign policy, it seems clear that accession to power of Islamist parties would represent a setback to both. Islamism calls for unity of church and state and for the enforcement of religious law. Although Islam may not be fundamentally incompatible with democracy, Islamism is because it holds that a majority of citizens cannot change rules established by God.[22] An extreme antidemocratic example is the Islamic Salvation Front in Algeria, which participated in elections during the early 1990s but whose leaders pledged that if it were elected and took office it would abolish future elections because they were incompatible with their interpretation of Islam. One of the leaders warned, "When we are in power, there will be no more elections because God will be ruling."[23]

Islamist groups have also adopted repressive and "antiwestern" policies once in power. For example, Sudan's Islamic, ethnically Arab government has pursued what amounts to a policy of ethnic cleansing and genocide against the non-Arab population of Darfur, a province of western Sudan that is the size of France. The Taliban in Afghanistan banned "music, picnics, wedding parties, pet birds, paper bags, the wearing of white socks, the shaving of beards, magazines, newspapers, most books, and children's toys."[24] Women were not allowed to attend school and for a time were even prohibited from leaving their homes unescorted and were restricted in their access to medical services.[25] Like the Sudan government, the Taliban government in Afghanistan conducted ethnic cleansing against minorities. An example occurred in 1999 when the Taliban government used military force to displace 10,000 Tajiks from a valley near the capital city. The crops and homes of the Tajiks were burned, and many of the Tajiks were subsequently arrested for "anti-Islamic" practices.[26] The Taliban also coerced children into military service, practiced torture, and executed citizens for their religious beliefs. (The anti-Tajik military operation, the repressive social regulations, and the harsh forms of "justice" confirm a point made elsewhere in this book: after the Taliban consolidated its hold on power in Kabul, Afghanistan was plainly not a "failed state," one that was physically unable to deliver essential public services. The Taliban did deliver services to the public, but not the kind of services normally expected of a modern government.)

The result in both Sudan and Afghanistan was diplomatic isolation, economic depression, and an absence of foreign investment—conditions that would clearly hobble a government's ability to manage the problems of the emerging megacity. There are Islamist factions throughout the fevered crescent and beyond into the Philippines. Outside of Iran, their prospects for actually assuming power appear at present to be confined largely to certain Arab segments of the crescent.

The states of the fevered crescent cannot afford more instability as they struggle to manage their overcrowded cities. It would be a bitter irony if in promoting what is undeniably a superior form of national governance in the long term, the United States and its allies inadvertently compromised the ability of those states to manage the problems taking shape in the so-called urban agglomerations.

The Prospects

How realistic are the prospects for democracy promotion in the fevered crescent, which is, after all, predominately Muslim? At the western tip of the arc, half of the population of Nigeria is Muslim, and at the eastern end is Indonesia, a state with a larger Muslim population than any other country in the world. A noted scholar of at least part of the Muslim world has observed a fundamental dilemma in the exportation of values by the figurative North to the figurative South, to use the terms of the "haves/have nots" dichotomy. Béchir Chourou of the University of Carthage–Tunis has concluded that the North-South encounter—whether one considers the opening of markets through economic reforms or the opening of societies through democratic change—has not been founded on a basis of mutual trust and confidence. The North lacks credibility in the South, having a longer history of intervention and control than cooperation in the region. Meanwhile, the South lacks legitimacy in the North, since so much of it lacks sound traditions of elected assemblies, separation of church and state, strong state-centric (rather than ethnic or tribal) identities, gender equality, or transparent and accessible governance.[27]

The democracy dilemma will be a central, if not the defining, issue for the fevered crescent states in coming years. In retrospect, Samuel Huntington's cautious 1968 articulation arguing for "consensus, community, legitimacy, organization, effectiveness, [and] stability" rather than President Bush's one-size-fits-all "distinctly American internationalism" is the more sensible and pragmatic solution.

Adaptive Democracy

To avoid the dangers inherent in aggressive democracy promotion, a long-term strategy of "adaptive democracy" should be gradual, blending old and new forms and avoiding drastic reforms that unsettle efforts to manage the expanding needs of the city. The acceptance of the traditional features of the *loya jirga* election in Afghanistan is an example. Another is the "split the difference" approach toward Islamic holy law that some Middle Eastern states (for example, Egypt and Syria) have taken whereby civil law is based upon Western models, and personal or family law is tied closely to the Qu'ran.

A system such as this might be more palatable (and hence more practical) in the short term than a fully secular code. Another example of splitting the difference with respect to the role of religion could be a federal approach under which provinces with more traditional cultures would have the autonomy to craft personal-family legal codes that are more sharia-oriented than those in other provinces. This is an approach that Nigeria has adopted.

As adaptive democracy begins to take root in various places, we may find that the "Muslim world" is as much a euphemism as the "West" and the "international community" are, and that one size never will fit all. There is now a sad recognition that the United States and its allies may have squandered the decade following the cold war by "talking the talk" but not "walking the walk" about democracy and open societies. We urge a democracy for the arc that will truly take root because it belongs there. Thus we must listen most to the voices—both frightening and promising—that arise from that region. And while we certainly do not agree that "benign despotism" is a proper model, we do agree that individual states and peoples within them will need to adapt in various, sometimes dissimilar, degrees.

It may be fruitful to consider how democracy will thrive in the fevered crescent, especially as liberalism has shifted and may be in permanent decline. John Lukacs, for example, has sharply noted:

> If liberal means the extension of all kinds of liberties to all kinds of individuals, these have now been institutionalized in unexpected and even astonishing ways. People throughout the world now benefit from freedom of which, less than a century ago, even the most radical liberals would not have dreamed. . . . At the same time, political and ideological liberalism has weakened, here and there even flickering out. . . .

The main business of the United States Congress has long been conducted not on the floor but in committees. . . . Meanwhile, the rights of
minorities (and of individuals) depend on the publicity they and their
advocates are able to produce to gain support among the otherwise
indifferent lawgivers.[28]

Materialism, conspicuous consumption, and the acquisition of material possession seem to empower large bureaucracies that "protect" possession and
slow the advancement of liberal causes such as "privacy, liberty, family, and
personal independence."[29] So, too, within the fevered crescent, we may well
witness political and constitutional phenomena driven by religion, tradition,
language, culture, and historical animosities and historical ties—rather than
idealistic, but Western, interpretations of values typically associated with
democracy. This being the case, the United States and the West in general
should not be surprised that emergent forms of democracy—if that best-
case scenario should manifest itself—will differ extraordinarily from the expectations that were initially offered when the tide of change began to take
hold in the fevered crescent.

Democracy, like a biological species, naturally evolves or mutates over
time in ways that optimize its "fit" with the enduring environmental conditions it faces. This is a phenomenon that ought to be supported, not resisted,
because it offers the best hope for positive and lasting change in a very troubled part of the world.

Foreign Policy Implications

The practice of foreign policy national security strategy has sometimes been described as being analogous to a board game or a sport. Former national security adviser Zbigniew Brzezinski, for example, called his 1997 book on strategy *The Grand Chessboard*. The British and Russian competition for influence in Central Asia during the nineteenth century and the more recent interventions by the United States in the oil-rich Persian Gulf region have both been referred to as the "great game." In truth, the making of strategy is analogous to a game in the sense that there are players (states, international organizations, nonstate actors) who move pieces (armed forces, foreign policy commitments, nonmilitary aid and technical assistance programs, investments) on a board (the globe) in order to maintain the status quo, alter the status quo in a favorable way, or minimize the impact of unfavorable changes in the status quo. The security challenges of the twenty-first century will require us to think differently about how to play the game.

The single most important element in the status quo—the element that strategists most wish to affect through the playing of the game—is the distribution of political, military, and economic power among states. For many years there was a near-exclusive emphasis on states as the players in the strategy game. As long as states owned or controlled the most important political, military, and economic playing pieces, it made sense to focus on the state. In fact, states still do control the most important game pieces, but other nonstate actors have begun to acquire game pieces that can no longer be discounted. In this context a state is a body politic whose government is recognized as a legal entity that exercises sovereignty over a defined territory and over the people who reside in that territory.

Since the early 1990s, it has often been thought that the centrality of the state in the strategy game has been diminished by the rise in power of international organizations such as the United Nations, the European Union, and the World Trade Organization and by the omnipresence of financial markets that allow economic resources to be shifted around the globe independently of any government. Nonstate actors such as multinational corporations, the press, and nongovernmental organizations such as the International Committee of the Red Cross and Amnesty International also chip away at the predominance of the state by virtue of their ability to shift assets across borders and mobilize public opinion in many different states in support of or in opposition to the policy preferences of the leaders of a state. Despite these factors, it nevertheless remains true that states continue to be the most important players because they have virtually exclusive control over the most powerful problem-solving assets in the strategy game—for example, foreign aid budgets, armed forces, government bureaucracies that do not need to generate a profit and therefore can be used to develop public infrastructure at home and abroad, central banks and mints, licensing authority over import access to domestic markets, and regulatory authority over exports to foreign markets.

Many of the problems—particularly international terrorism—that states will be called upon to solve in the future will arise in and around the megacities that are mushrooming in the fevered crescent. The sheer magnitude of the challenges that will be posed across the Lagos-Cairo-Karachi-Jakarta arc will exceed the capacity of any one state, including the United States, to resolve. Success at meeting these challenges will require cooperation among states and other actors in the international community, but the grand strategies that have been proposed in recent years for organizing interstate cooperation are not well suited for the challenges of the twenty-first century.

Furthermore, homeland security programs will inhibit cooperation with some states under any strategic design. Homeland security programs are inherently national—they emphasize more effective controls over and restrictions of the people and goods that cross national borders, strengthened domestic intelligence and law enforcement, as well as emergency preparedness programs that seek to minimize the domestic consequences of terrorist attacks. Cooperative and collaborative approaches have, of course, been developed to balance homeland security precautions against the facilitation of trade and travel between neighboring states and among major trading partners. For example, the United States and Canada cooperate on border controls, and the United States and Western European states collaborate on joint cargo inspection and certification regimes. Such arrangements work because the administrative capabilities of the partners are similar enough to warrant each to rely upon the other.

Many states will, however, be unable to meet the administrative expectations that the United States will, and indeed should, demand of a partner. As a result, homeland security programs may cause a reduction in all sorts of interchange with nonpartner states. The result will be lower levels of immigration from nonpartner states into the United States; fewer tourists, guest workers, and exchange students from those states; and tighter controls on cargoes shipped from or even through those states. There will also be less foreign investment in the economies of those states because the economic prospects in the global market will be lower than the prospects of partner states. This in turn will make effective cooperation with these states on addressing the problems of the twenty-first century—problems from which we cannot really isolate ourselves in the global economy—considerably more complex and difficult to organize.

Homeland security may also complicate international cooperation by narrowing the scope of governmental spending patterns. Because of terrorist attacks, the United States has been forced to invest billions of dollars in baggage screening at airports, improved immigration and customs systems, emergency preparedness, and other homeland security projects. Before September 11, 2001, the United States budgeted about $17 billion at the federal level for homeland security; in 2003 the homeland security budget was $43 billion.[1] In the context of huge government deficits, every dollar that is spent on homeland security is in effect a dollar that cannot be spent on addressing the problems of overpopulation, undergovernance, and slow economic growth overseas.

Interstate Cooperation Strategies

Trial lawyers often refer to a "theory of the case" around which they organize their research, marshal evidence, and prepare the list of witnesses they plan on calling for testimony. The theory is always subject to change, as when a key witness changes testimony or dramatic new evidence is introduced by the other side. In a sense, today's strategists resemble lawyers who have been presented with dramatic new evidence. The most vivid—but hardly the only—evidence is in postwar Iraq where America's semi-unilateralism has proven to be too costly and politically divisive inside NATO and within the American body politic. Other evidence calling for new theories of the case for interstate cooperation is emerging, as we demonstrated in the preceding chapters, from overpopulated and undergoverned zones in the fevered crescent.

U.S. strategy under the Bush administration is often labeled unilateralist particularly with regard toward Iraq. This is not an entirely accurate label. The unilateralist theory of the case is that interstate cooperation is not important enough to warrant compromise over goals or important timetables and that the state—the United States in this case—can sometimes serve its national interests best by going it alone. Strictly speaking, that is not what the Bush administration's strategy has been in Iraq or elsewhere.

With respect to Iraq, a coalition did exist, there were attempts to secure UN and NATO support for the war, and compromises were offered to facilitate postwar reconstruction. That having been said, it is nevertheless true that the United States was obviously willing to proceed with a relatively small coalition and without the kind of political support from the United Nations and NATO that a multilateralist might have regarded as a prerequisite.

The problems of the future will inescapably require multilateral solutions, and, of course, the states from which we expect the highest value cooperation are states that are similar to the United States in values, interests, and financial resources. In other words, the states in the figurative winners' circle of advanced economies in Western Europe, North America, and East Asia are the ones with whom it makes the most sense to work. The strategic problem is that the national security and human security issues arising from the Lagos-Cairo-Karachi-Jakarta arc and in other less developed parts of the world will require more resources than will be available at any one time and from any one source. Some form of prioritization will be required—and to maximize effectiveness, the prioritization scheme should be a common one, shared by all cooperating states.

Three theories for prioritizing effort in addressing security, economic, and governance problems in countries outside the figurative winners' circle have been advocated in recent years, and none are suitable for the twenty-first century. Each is considered below.

The Failed State Theory

This theory supposes that the most effective and efficient approach to solving security, economic, and governance problems in less developed countries is to focus attention on the locations where the problems are worst. This theory calls for strategies that focus international effort on investing money and solving the problems of so-called failed states.

In the 1990s, failed states were singled out for attention by academics and humanitarian activists because they were the source of egregious violence against civilians, gross human rights abuses, widespread starvation and disease, and destabilizing outflows of refugees to neighboring states. After the September 11 terrorist attacks, the argument that failed states deserved priority attention was broadened. After the United States committed to fighting a war on terrorism, failed states began to be identified as being likely launching pads and safe havens for terrorist groups.

There is, however, no single definition of the term *failed state*, and many of the definitions that have been offered are overly broad. For example, some definitions include states that had simply ceased to exist and had since been succeeded by another state or states. In fact, this is the definition that was adopted by the U.S. government's State Failure Task Force. The task force was commissioned by the Clinton administration during the 1990s to identify the causes of state failure in order to improve the government's ability to predict and prevent future state failures. Although the state failures it was trying to prevent were humanitarian catastrophes such as the famine cum clan warfare in Somalia, the definition that the Task Force adopted was so broad that it included the Austro-Hungarian Empire as a failed state because the territory that had once been administered as a single, unified entity by the Hapsburgs had been replaced by successor states after World War I. By this standard the successor states of Yugoslavia and Czechoslovakia are also failures, because they too were replaced by new states in the 1990s.

For the purposes of designing strategies for prioritizing international effort in the future, such an expansive definition is useless. For one thing, state failure of the Austro-Hungarian type is often not something that should be guarded against. Some state failures of this type are positive in terms of U.S. national interests, and they benefit human security interests, as when state failure frees captive nationalities or when the failure reflects the desires of the citizenry. The former was the case with the failure of the Soviet Union, which enabled the Baltic States to regain independence; the latter was the case when the people of Czechoslovakia decided to divide themselves into the Czech Republic and Slovakia. State failure can also be positive in terms of the war on terrorism when a state sponsor of terrorism fails or is made to fail, as was the case with the Taliban regime in Afghanistan, or when the failure of an oppressive state brings an end to repressive conditions that may have sparked domestic terrorism or international terrorism against the allies of the oppressive state. An example of the latter is the presence of Saudi nationals in the radical, anti-American Islamist movements.

The State Failure Task Force complicated the matter by broadening the definition even further by including governmental "shifts away from democracy and towards authoritarian rule" as a type of state failure.[2] In a sense, of course, it is true that authoritarianism represents a failure—a failure in the sense that by abandoning democratic practices the state would be failing to adhere to widely accepted standards of good governance. In terms of strategy, however, this definition mixes apples and oranges. This may be acceptable for a comparative analysis of political change, but it offers a poor guide to strategic thinking about a contemporary issue. Adoption of an authoritarian style of government is the exact opposite of the type of state failure that occurred in Somalia. Somalia was characterized by too little government, and the evidence of its failure was chaotic civil disorder, widespread famine, and a government that did not resist waves of international intervention. Authoritarianism could hardly be more different. Authoritarian regimes are ordinarily characterized by heavy-handed government, forceful repression of dissent and disorder, and prickly assertion of the right of sovereignty.

Other definitions of failed states are narrower and consequently have more practical utility than the State Failure Task Force's approach, although none are satisfactory as guidelines for the kinds of issues that will arise in the future. These other definitions are keyed to the ability or inability of the central government at the national level to carry out its basic functions. While there is no unanimity about exactly what basic functions a state must be unable to perform in order to deserve the failed state label, there is a consensus that any state that is unable to prevent persistent, widespread civil disorder within its boundaries and is unable to defend its borders or represent itself to other governments is ipso facto a failed state.[3] Indeed, the State Failure Task Force would also recognize such a state as having failed. These common denominators of failed state definitions are, however, difficult to apply in practice—and if they cannot be applied consistently in practice, they are of little practical value.

For example, in September 2004 a joint study by the Argentine Navy's Center for Strategic Studies, the Alexis de Tocqueville Center for Hemispheric Studies in Buenos Aires, and the U.S. Naval War College published an analysis of the failed state phenomenon in South America that adopted the common denominator definition. The study referred to Colombia as a "failing state" but not a failed state in the sense that Afghanistan and Somalia were. Apparently recognizing the imprecision of the label, the authors also characterized Colombia as a "nearly failed state" and a "victim state with only some of the characteristics of a failed state."[4] As will be discussed below, the study's reference to Somalia and Afghanistan as the quintessential failed states was also misguided, as Somalia in the early 1990s and Afghanistan in the early 2000s were vastly different in terms of their status.

Before September 11, states that were unable to contain civil disorder were of concern to strategists and foreign policy experts because of the humanitarian consequences of disorder and because disorder was often regionally destabilizing, as when large numbers of refugees flee the disorder and unsettle neighboring states (for example, the Rwandans who fled to Zaire in 1994) or when neighboring states decide to take advantage of the disorder by intervening directly or indirectly through client militias. After September 11, there was also concern that the states that were unable to contain disorder were becoming platforms for international terrorist groups. For example, former National Security Council aide Susan E. Rice wrote that failed states "often do serve as safe havens and staging grounds for terrorist organizations."[5] Robert I. Rotberg of the Kennedy School's Program on Intrastate Conflict and Conflict Resolution and the president of the World Peace Foundation agreed that failed states have become both "reservoirs and exporters of terror."[6] Other observers saw failed states in Africa as being particularly likely to become springboards for international terrorism in the future.[7]

There is more than logical supposition behind the argument that terrorist groups may see opportunity in failed states. There is evidence that terrorist groups have, indeed, taken advantage of state failure. There have been reports that al-Qaeda has engaged in diamond smuggling in two failed states (Sierra Leone and the Democratic Republic of Congo) in order to raise funds.[8] There have also been reports that al-Qaeda has conducted some operations out of bases in another failed state, Somalia.[9] The U.S. State Department's *Patterns of Global Terrorism Report* for 2003 indicates that active al-Qaeda elements continue to be present in Somalia.[10]

The specific concern is that terrorist groups with global reach will be able to establish and maintain bases of operation in failed states. Unfortunately, in the twenty-first century few terrorists groups will lack international, if not global reach. Economic globalization with its growing trade flows and ever-expanding international transportation networks make travel inexpensive. Tools for cross-border communications are readily available in even the most remote locations, thus terrorist leaders in Central Asia can provide direction to cells in Europe and North America.

It does not, however, follow that the best strategy is for the United States and its allies to orchestrate an international effort to resurrect and reinvigorate the class of failed states. For such a strategy to succeed in addressing the problems of the future, failed states as a class would have to be clearly definable. As has been noted above, a single, clear definition has been elusive, and many of the policy proposals for dealing with failed states actually complicate the problem by discussing failed, failing, and weak states as if they should all be part of the same class. A class that included all three groups of states might constitute most of the states outside the winners' circle of North America and Western Europe. This would hardly be an effective approach to prioritizing international effort. Moreover, the problems posed by genuinely failed states—such as Somalia and the Democratic Republic of Congo where the government has at one time or another conclusively demonstrated its inability to prevent, contain, or suppress widespread civil disorder—are qualitatively different from the problems presented by states whose governments are "only" weak.

A second condition is that failed states as a class would have to be a more likely source of regional instability, economic disruption, human insecurity, and terrorism than other classes of states. It seems clear that failed states as a class, whether narrowly or broadly defined, do not meet this condition. For one thing, as has been noted, the locus of the most serious problems will be in the functioning states of the Lagos-Cairo-Karachi-Jakarta arc, not in failed states outside that arc. With respect to terrorism, the answer is less clear, but upon close inspection, the argument that failed states as a class are better platforms or more secure safe havens for terrorist groups does not hold up. The facts seem to be that failed states are no more hospitable to the terrorist groups that threaten the United States and its allies than other groups of states—such as weak states or, for that matter, strong or even allied states. Indeed, the evidence suggests that the more dangerous terrorist threats have emanated from states that have not actually failed. Further, many "consensus failed states" (Somalia, Haiti) affect relatively small populations in comparison with the urbanizing states along the fevered crescent and have scant effect on regional economies.

Failed States and Terrorism

The U.S. Commission on National Security in the Twenty-first Century (also known as the Hart-Rudman Commission) is justifiably renowned for having highlighted in 1999 and 2000 America's vulnerability to attacks from sub-state terrorist groups. It also predicted that failed states would continue to be a problem in the future. But failed states were not identified by the Commission as being a particularly important platform for terrorist activities.[11] In fact, in Phase II of the Commission's work, it emphasized that the primary concerns with failed states were humanitarian.[12]

The Commission's judgment appears to have been confirmed by data about the identity of the individuals who were engaged in major terrorist events. It has often been noted that most of the September 11 terrorists were Saudi, but Saudi Arabia was not then and is not now regarded as a failed state. Whatever its failings in the human rights arena, the Saudi government has demonstrated its ability to contain and suppress civil disorder. Some of the planning for September 11 was apparently undertaken by cells of operatives in Germany, another state that hardly qualifies as failed. The operatives who planned and conducted the March 2004 train bombings in Madrid were based in Morocco and Spain itself, neither of which have been identified by any scholars or strategists as being a failed state. The 2002 terrorist bombing in Bali was apparently perpetrated by an Indonesian group; some experts believe that Indonesia could become a failed state in the future, but it has not yet been identified as such.[13]

Afghanistan is a particularly illuminating case in point. Even before September 11, it was widely recognized that al-Qaeda had major bases of operation in Afghanistan, but it was not considered a failed state at the time. In fact, to the extent that a loose organization such as al-Qaeda can be said to have had a headquarters, al-Qaeda's was in Afghanistan until the Taliban was toppled in 2001–2002. Al-Qaeda's infrastructure (training camps, arms caches, equipment depots) in Afghanistan was both extensive and widely known. The extent of the infrastructure is precisely why in August 1998 the United States attempted to kill al-Qaeda leadership and disrupt its operations by launching cruise missile attacks against its sites in Afghanistan. However, even according to the State Failure Task Force's expansive definition of failure, Afghanistan was not considered a failed state at the time the attacks were undertaken. Nor was it considered a failed state in the two years after the attack and before the date that the Task Force's report was issued.[14]

The Afghanistan example suggests important implications about the role that aid to failed states should play in the war on terrorism. Under the Taliban, Afghanistan made itself into an international pariah by virtue of its medieval cultural and social policies and its vindictiveness toward other religions, not because its government was incapable of containing domestic disorder. If anything, the Taliban government distinguished itself by its heavy-handedness, such as its Nazi-esque requirement that non-Muslims wear external identification tags.

In fact, the very inabilities of failed states make them unreliable providers of protection and infrastructure. Regimes that exert little control over internal security forces will not be able to provide protection for terrorist base camps against rival terrorist factions or local insurgents. Moreover, failed states may well be viewed by terrorists as being unable to provide more than token resistance to antiterrorist incursions by neighboring states or by special operations units from western states. Failed states may even be seen by terrorist organizations as incapable of distinguishing between antiterrorist incursions and indigenous violence—and thus as being unable or unwilling to even offer a stout verbal defense of their legal sovereignty at the UN, in regional organizations such as the African Union, or in the court of international public opinion. The Taliban might have failed to improve the living conditions in Afghanistan, but they did control enough of the country to make al-Qaeda view the Taliban government as a sound strategic partner—one that would be able to assert claims of state sovereignty at the United Nations and the Organization of the Islamic Conference and also provide greater protection to terrorist training camps and weapons caches than could be found in the chaos of a Sierra Leone or Somalia. Indeed, the Taliban's assertion of its rights as the rulers of Afghanistan underlay its refusal to turn over al-Qaeda leadership to the United States after September 11. This refusal, of course, was the regime's death knell.

Another consideration is that the government agencies of failed states are not well connected with Western intelligence sources and thus their employees may never be in a position to obtain and leak advance warning of impending counterterror operations to resident terrorist groups. Corrupt employees of functioning states are clearly in a better position than employees of failed states to provide this sort of intelligence support to terrorist groups.

Fund-raising by terrorist organizations is another aspect of this issue. As noted above, terrorist organizations have financed some operations through criminal activity in failed states. Clearly, anything that enables groups like al-Qaeda to finance their operations and fund their weapons purchases ought to be of substantial concern to strategists, but this problem is not peculiar to failed states. While smuggling is considerably easier in a state that exerts no control over its borders, goods are routinely smuggled out of functioning states (e.g., diamonds from Tanzania, drugs from Colombia, small arms from Russia), and the profits from these enterprises can be used to finance terrorism. For that matter, criminal enterprises inside functioning states can also generate funds for terrorists. Even in the United States, terrorist operatives or their sympathizers have engaged in illegal activity (such as smuggling cigarettes from low tax states for resale in high tax states, embezzling from Muslim charities, and extorting money from legitimate businessmen and families) in order to raise funds for terrorism.

The bottom line is that failed states are a matter of continuing concern, but in terms of strategy to combat terrorism they appear not to warrant special attention as a class of states. There is no compelling evidence to suggest that failed states present substantially better platforms for basing, training, and fund-raising by terrorist groups than other states. Indeed, as we have noted, some discussions of the failed state phenomenon implicitly concede this point by discussing failed, failing, and weak states as if they were a homogeneous class of states.

The Buffer States Theory

This theory supposes that the United States and its allies can protect themselves against the threats of the twenty-first century by helping other key states to strengthen their military, intelligence, law enforcement, and anti-terror capabilities. In effect, the theory envisions threats as emanations from the far side of a figurative cordon sanitaire of capable buffer states.

Buffer state strategies have long been a part of the strategy game. For example, after World War II, the Soviet Union established a column of buffer states between it and Western Europe. The buffer states were forced to fit into the Warsaw Pact in order to better insulate the core of the Soviet empire from sources of economic, cultural, and ideological contagion in the West and to serve as a shock absorber in the event of military attack during a conflict with NATO. Like the Soviet Union's Warsaw Pact satellites, buffer states typically occupy territory between a state that perceives a potential threat and the state or states from which a threat is posed. Since there are no threatening states north of Canada or south of Mexico, the traditional buffer state strategy has not figured heavily in the game plan of North American strategists. Some Russian observers view U.S. involvement in Central Asia as providing a buffer for Russia against Islamic extremism.[15]

Mexico has, however, been thought of as a buffer in the context of constricting the flow of illegal immigrants from Central American states (and, of course, from Mexico itself). This conception of a buffer state as a filter or screen has, like the failed states strategy, had new life breathed into it by the war on terror. It is being applied with varying degrees of success in both North America and Europe. The European Union, for example, is encouraging neighboring states (in Northern Africa and Eastern Europe) to adopt and enforce stricter standards on immigration, on the assumption that terrorists would otherwise migrate through the neighboring states into Europe.

A more elegant and expansive adaptation of the buffer state strategy envisions the world as being split between two camps and seeks to use key states along the dividing lines or "seams" between the two camps as buffers. One camp contains the developed and near-developed world; the second and smaller camp consists of those states that have not participated in economic globalization out of choice (Islamist regimes) or misfortune (failed states, weak states). As a consequence, states in the second camp are theoretically populated with disaffected leaders and disadvantaged (and often highly disaffected) citizens. It is from the geographic areas populated by these disaffected leaders and peoples that the threats of tomorrow are presumed to emerge. The threats may be from a state (North Korea), a group sponsored by a state (Hizbullah), or terrorists acting completely independently of a state (al-Qaeda)—but in each instance the threat is seen to be emanating from inside the camp of the disadvantaged and disaffected states.[16]

In a sense the seams between the developed and disaffected camps resemble the fault lines between civilizations or cultures that were envisioned by Professor Samuel Huntington in the early 1990s.[17] Huntington saw the fault lines as principally reflecting fundamental cultural and religious differences among the worldviews of "peoples." The seams drawn in the new buffer state strategy represent divides among states with fundamentally different approaches to secular issues such as economic globalization, free enterprise, and individual rights. Given the pervasiveness of immigration over the past decades (there are, for example, more Lebanese Arabs in Brazil than in Lebanon itself), Huntington's conception of cultural differences that strictly parallel geographic boundaries and his notion that the friction and threats are concentrated along those boundaries are open to challenge.

The key assumption in buffer state strategies is that a select number of key states on the seams or along the cultural divide can actually provide some sort of physical barrier or filter against threats emanating from the camp of the disconnected and disaffected. Indeed, one proposal designates the 12 most important buffer states as Mexico, Brazil, South Africa, Morocco, Algeria, Greece, Turkey, Pakistan, Thailand, Malaysia, the Philippines, and Indonesia. Under this proposal, each of these 12 would get priority attention from the United States and other first camp states in terms of economic, political, and military assistance in order to help them serve more effectively as barriers against terrorist networks.[18]

Some of the 12 key buffer states seem particularly ill-suited for the role the strategy envisions for them. Pakistan, Indonesia, and the Philippines have long ago demonstrated their inability to assert effective control over remote rural areas and to police their expansive borders and coastlines—a sine qua non, one would think, of an effective buffer state. Although there are as yet no signs that Brazil is home to major terrorist groups, there are serious questions about the extent of Brazil's effective control over its remote interior sections, in particular near the western borders with Colombia and Peru and the southern borderlands with Paraguay and Argentina.[19] As every homeowner knows, window screens with holes in them are not effective at keeping mosquitoes out of the house. Further, one must wonder whether the lesson of the multiyear effort to capture or kill Osama bin Laden in the Pakistan-Afghanistan border region is that it is physically impossible to patch all the holes in the screens.

Another problem with the strategy is that terrorist organizations have already succeeded in establishing cells and bases of operation in the prospective buffer states. Ultimately, there is little reason to suppose that even if all 12 key states were strengthened as buffers, no new terrorist cells would form in Algiers, Rabat, Hamburg, Toulon, or, for that matter, Detroit. States designated as buffers may indeed deserve assistance and may also desire strong relations with the United States. The question, though, for American strategists is whether strengthening buffer states will materially improve the security of the United States against terrorism or other threats. It seems clear that the answer is no.

As long as commercial airlines routinely fly to places like Kabul and Khartoum and cargo ships move between ports on both sides of the proposed *cordon sanitaire*, terrorist organizations will be able to fly over or sail around whatever barriers the seam states like Mexico might provide. Moreover, in terms of the defensive aspects of the war, homeland security is better served by investment in customs and immigration systems at points of entry in the United States—systems that will reduce interactions with some of the states where human security problems are worst and where terrorism and disorder will continue to grow—than in improving the buffer-filter capacity of states that do not share a border with us.

In terms of the broader social and human security issues that may destabilize broad swathes of the globe, buffer states' strategies have little to offer. They are defensive and reactive at a time when a proactive, multilateral strategy is required.

The Pivotal States Theory

This theory envisions a more proactive approach on the part of the United States and a select number of other states. The select states are regional pivots—states that are so economically, politically, and militarily dominant in their respective regions that they shape events regionwide. The pivotal states strategy aims leverage their regional influence through prioritized investment, foreign aid, and other forms of state-to-state assistance and political support. In effect, foreign aid and spending by the United States would, under this strategy, be wheeled away from less dominant states in order to make more money available for investment in and assistance to more dominant ones. The theory was that regional stability would result if pivotal states became more stable and prosperous and became more closely aligned with the United States.[20] The success of such a strategy obviously depends upon the ability of statesmen to correctly identify the pivots and then for the U.S.

government to focus aid and other forms of assistance on the pivots at the expense of less dominant states.

Although one could argue that the heavy U.S. investment in nation-building and security operations in Iraq and Afghanistan amounts to a de facto judgment that Iraq and Afghanistan are pivotal states, this investment actually demonstrates how impractical the pivotal state strategy has turned out to be. It also illustrates some inherent obstacles to all prioritization schemes that group states into categories for consistent and long-term policy treatment.

First of all, even though huge amounts are being invested there, neither Iraq nor Afghanistan is pivotal in the sense originally intended. Neither Iraq nor Afghanistan was regionally dominant in the 1990s, and neither is regionally dominant today. In fact, by most objective measures, Iraq and Afghanistan are among the least important states in the Southwest and Central Asia regions. Their population, economic throw-weight, and geographic size pale in comparison with other states in the region. Iran, for example, is considerably larger than Iraq and Afghanistan combined in terms of territory, population, and gross domestic product. By any standard, India, Turkey, Saudi Arabia, Iran, and Pakistan are vastly more important actors than Afghanistan and Iraq in terms of projecting influence in the Southwest and Central Asia regions. In fact, given the problems that the fledgling Iraqi and Afghan governments currently face in establishing control over their own territory, it is decidedly unlikely that either will ever occupy a more prominent position in terms of regional influence than some of their neighbors.

It is true that in both instances, one of the primary arguments for continuing to invest in nation-building is that events in Iraq and Afghanistan will help set the direction of the Greater Near East. This is certainly a valid argument, but it is not the argument that the pivotal states strategy makes. In fact, Iraq and Afghanistan demonstrate that events and political considerations inevitably influence, if not entirely determine, decisions about where a state invests its diplomatic energies and foreign assistance monies. The United States is investing in Afghanistan and Iraq not because these states fell into a particular category of states that had been predesignated for special handling over the long term but because events drove it to do so. As important as it is to stabilize the situations in both countries, it must be noted that the effort of providing stability contributes little to solving the security problems percolating in the future.

The world is a complicated place, perhaps now more than ever. It is understandable that the people responsible for playing the foreign policy and security strategy game would want to simplify it and thus make it more man-

ageable and easier to explain to the voters. In a democracy where funding
for foreign policy initiatives is heavily dependent upon public perceptions
of interests and threats to those interests, the desirability and utility of easy-
to-understand strategy explanations should not be underestimated. In truth
there is a surface logic to the proposition that states with similar characteristics deserve similar treatment by diplomats and strategists. Indeed, throughout the cold war both the United States and the Soviet Union did just that.
States were grouped into categories based largely upon their ideological
dispositions. Each superpower tended to see the world as being divided
into three camps, or groups of states: allies, neutrals, and adversaries. This
approach worked because the division was largely declaratory. Most states
declared their status—for example, by affiliating with the nonaligned movement or formally joining one of several alliance structures (for example, the
North Atlantic Treaty Organization, the Organization of American States,
the Southeast Asia Treaty Organization, and, on the Soviet side, the Warsaw
Pact and COMINTERN). The bipolarity of the cold war and alliance structures also forced many states to sublimate the internal tensions they faced
and the interstate rivalries in the name of the greater threat, world war, or
domination by the "other" superpower. For the foreseeable future, there will
be no second pole and thus no reason for many states to either declare their
status or mean it. (Islamists would counter that there are still two poles or
camps: the zone occupied by Muslims and the zone occupied by everyone
else.)

This is not to say that there is no value to consistency when it comes to
strategy and diplomacy in the fog of the post–cold war era. Oscar Wilde
surely overstated the case when he labeled consistency as the refuge of un-
imaginative minds. But consistency is not an end in and of itself, and there
are risks to consistency if it results in misallocation of effort. This is, unfortunately, the signal flaw of various proposals for strategies based upon the
categorization of states, be they failed, buffer, or pivotal states. Or allied
states, for that matter.

Terrorism is not the only aspect of this issue, but it is certainly one of the
central security challenges of the future. With respect to any effort to deal
with terrorism, the problem with grouping states into categories and designing category-specific foreign and security policies is that the vast majority of
states simply do not fit in any single category.

As this chapter has sought to demonstrate, the term *failed states* is so
amorphous as to be useless as a tool for formulating foreign policies. Moreover, it is highly likely that even if a precise definition could be agreed upon,

the nations of the world would be exceedingly reluctant to designate individual states as failed states because of the precedent that might set for international intervention. The exceptions would be the extremely rare cases of a national government simply ceasing to exist or a state formally declaring itself as having failed. Neither scenario is likely as long as there are powerful elements in the state that can benefit from control—even nominal control—over the government, or as long as there are other states concerned about giving the UN or a group of Western powers license to take over a fellow state that has not formally relinquished its claim to sovereignty.

Further, many functioning states have characteristics of failed states, and many healthy states with strong economies have provided platforms for terrorism. Indeed, even allied states in the most economically advanced regions of the world have served, unwittingly, as bases for terrorist cells. As we know, some of the cells that supported the September 11 al-Qaeda attacks on the United States were operating out of Germany, which is an ally of the United States and has one of the most advanced economies in the world. The phenomenon of terrorist basing in Western Europe is not, of course, a new phenomenon. The Red Brigades and other radical terrorists operated in Western Europe during the 1960s, 1970s, and early 1980s.

With respect to functioning states with characteristics of failed states, examples abound. There are, for example, ungoverned rural areas in the tribal zones along both sides of the border between Afghanistan and Pakistan, isolated valleys in the functioning states of the Caucasus, and the Yemeni outback. Substantial growth in the already overgrown populations of cities in states such as Nigeria, Pakistan, and Indonesia will only increase the number of undergoverned or completely ungoverned areas, even as it exacerbates human security and environmental problems that will draw the globe's attention even after the war on terrorism winds down.

A more effective approach to prioritizing state-to-state assistance for the war on terror is to do more of what we do not do enough of today—focus on fixing problems, not on organizing states into categories for common policy treatment. Foreign aid and other forms of state-to-state assistance should be based upon the recipient state's potential contribution to specific high-priority projects or functions in the war on terrorism: for example, the collection and sharing of intelligence information about terrorist organizations, law enforcement action against indigenous terrorist groups with affiliations to al-Qaeda, the suppression of illegal fund-raising activities by terrorist organizations, and effective regulation and monitoring of financial transfers that support terrorist organizations.

The same approach of concentrating effort on specific problems also ought to be applied to the other security challenges of the twenty-first century. As we have noted earlier, there are a wide range of human security problems that will be boiling over in the fevered crescent during this century. In the following—and final—chapter, we recommend ways of identifying, prioritizing, and addressing these specific problems.

A New Covenant

The first step in addressing the emerging challenges in and around the fevered crescent must be to generate awareness of the problems on the part of the actors that matter in the international system. The next steps are mobilizing this awareness into action and marshaling action in ways that may maximize positive results. Our use of the conditional "may" is deliberate; across-the-board success cannot be guaranteed. There are so many moving pieces in this puzzle that even the best orchestration of international effort may come up short in some locations. With this caveat in mind, in this concluding chapter we identify key actors and discuss ways to generate awareness and mobilize and marshal action.

As noted earlier, over the past two decades, there have been numerous ruminations on the decline of the state as the key actor and on the increase of the power and influence of nonstate actors. Among the nonstate actors once presumed to have gained prominence at the expense of states are international organizations such as the United Nations, multinational corporations, global markets, and nongovernment organizations.

For all its good intent, the United Nations has proven incapable of addressing many challenges—understandably, given its limited resources and the inability of its leading members to unite behind a common set of policies and priorities. Its inability to muster credible, meaningful action in the Rwanda genocide in 1994 and throughout the early, middle, and late stages of the genocide in Darfur, Sudan, illustrates how the conflicting agenda of member states enfeeble—and often hobble—the UN.

As countries such as India, Brazil, Egypt, and Japan clamor for permanent membership on the UN Security Council, the organization may weaken further. Without question, further "dilution" of Security Council identity—even one unquestionably more representative of global population and emerging powers—will lead to further intractability on issues crucial to the well-being of the planet.

This is not to say that Brazil or other emerging states do not have as great or greater a claim on permanent Security Council membership as some of the current permanent members. For example, India's population and economy are both significantly larger than France's. Brazil's population is three times as large as France's, and the Brazilian economy as measured by gross domestic product is already almost as large as the French economy and is certain to surpass it in the near future. Our point here is not that an adjustment in the composition of the "permanent five" is unwarranted, but rather that controversy over the membership of the permanent five will hamstring the United Nations and, even after it is resolved, will very likely introduce disabling tensions within the Security Council and the larger United Nations system.

The authors themselves are of two minds on the subject UN Security Council reform. Liotta tends to support multilateral decisions made by an organized body that more clearly represents the economic, cultural, and demographic forces of the future. By contrast, Miskel remains more pragmatic than idealistic regarding the potential value of such reforms. We agree that the introduction of new permanent Security Council members with veto powers might reintroduce the kind of ideological and political divisions that crippled the body during the cold war. India and China, for example, may turn out to be as wary of each other's motives as the United States and the Soviet Union were in the 1980s. If Egypt were to become a permanent member, it would likely conceive of itself as the voice of the Arab and Islamic worlds and thus be compelled by domestic and regional pressure to adopt a confrontational stance toward "Western" approaches to international issues. Moreover, like Brazil and some other potential Security Council members, Egypt does not have the kind of economic or "governance" surpluses that would enable it to export much more than rhetoric to the international effort that will be required to address the multipronged problems that will emanate from the fevered crescent.

The truth is that Egypt and Brazil and many other large and populous countries are struggling to manage internal challenges of slow economic growth, urbanization, pollution, civil disorder, and terrorism and are not in a position to export the investment funds and nation-building expertise that will be needed to help other nations solve their problems. It is true that Egypt, Brazil, and others are in a position to offer military peacekeepers, but as we have tried to make clear, the challenge is far from being exclusively military.

In other words, reform at the United Nations would introduce greater tensions inside the Security Council. States without exportable nation-building resources would have power equal to the states with the resources. The predictable result is that the nations with the resources will trim their commitments to the United Nations and the organization will become even less effective at its traditional functions.

The only place in the world where the United Nations has invested serious, multiyear energy in nation-building is Bosnia-Herzegovina, and the reason for Bosnia's favored status is that events there are understood by major powers to directly affect their national interests. It is, after all, unavoidable, largely salutary, and fully consistent with the basic democratic principle that citizens should have a voice in where national resources are spent that nations invest most heavily where their national interests are at stake.

The United Nations' most effective contribution to security in the twenty-first century may be to educate the people of the figurative "West"—the leaders and citizens of economically advanced and politically stable states—about where their true national interests will be in the future and about how these interests will be challenged by the developments we have described in this book. Educating leaders and citizens alike is a role in which the United Nations has succeeded in the past and can succeed in the future.

We have one particular example in mind: the United Nations Conference on the Human Environment, held in Stockholm in 1972. The conference itself was not a resounding success in that the problems and issues it addressed were, obviously, not resolved in the ensuing months. In fact, the problems still exist and may have only gotten worse due to the dramatic spread of industry since 1972. The conference was, however, successful in formulating new international approaches to global problems. It led to the permanent establishment of the United Nations Environment Programme (UNEP), which was the first UN organizational headquarters established in the so-called developing world. Today, UNEP serves a global environmental role, advocates for the "voiceless" by highlighting the disadvantages and needs of the emerging world, and (given its location in Nairobi) has been a focal point for leveraging political and civil disputes in neighboring Somalia and Sudan.

Further, the Declaration of the United Nations Conference on the Human Environment amounted to a recognition by UN members that the environment was a problem that transcended borders and as such would require national governments, local governments, civil society, industry, and the public in general to act together.[1] The outcome of the conference has been an effort to minimize future environmental degradation and remediate the environmental stresses of the past. UNEP today monitors the environment, mobilizes civil society's engagement on environmental issues, and educates government officials at all levels about environmental science and technology.

It is true that few environmental activists will be completely satisfied with the results to date, and the environmental stresses will worsen sharply in some parts of the world in the near future. But the Conference on the Human Environment did mobilize effort and spawn new approaches toward tackling environmental problems. Among the new approaches was the Clean Up the World campaign, begun in 1993. Under this program, each year communities in more than 100 countries participate in annual trash pickup, recycling, and similar activities. What is unique about the program beyond its scope is that it directly engages local communities and is sponsored by the United Nations and corporate donors. Other examples of collaborative projects spawned by the conference include seventeen partnership programs between neighboring states trying to reduce wastewater pollution in shared coastal zones. Another example is the collaborative effort with private sector financial institutions in eastern and central Europe that was started in 2004 to improve the banking industry's understanding of new environmental regulations and their effects upon lending practices.

These approaches may not be unique in the sense that nothing like them had ever before been attempted by a United Nations program. What is unique is the overall approach of an attention-getting conference followed by continuing work to mobilize public support (UNEP work groups and regional workshops and conferences) and collaborative efforts with industry, citizen groups, national governmental, subnational, municipal governments, and international organizations at the regional level. This sort of grand strategy is what will be required to address the crises emerging in the fevered crescent. The fact that the program is still adapting and developing flexible solutions is another reason why we have selected the UNEP as a model.

UNEP also seems a viable model because the Stockholm conference took place during the cold war, at a time when mobilizing international action was complicated by ideological division among the great powers. Today, as the problems in the feral cities and undergoverned areas of the fevered crescent grow, there is also a new ideological divide that must be overcome if genuine progress is to be made in tackling the security challenges of the twenty-first century. This is not quite the "North-South" or "haves vs. have nots" divide that many have predicted since the 1960s. The issue of disparity in living standards between the advanced economies of North America, Western Europe, and East Asia are, of course, very much a source of tension—but the ideological divide is between so-called Western standards (in general, free enterprise, globalization, rule of law, democratic forms of governance, and gender equality) and traditional, often Islamic cultural beliefs that reject the individualism and materialism of the West and at the same time serve as justification for the maintenance of an obsolete status quo by political, religious, and tribal elites who are seemingly incapable of providing the leadership their societies will need as their urban populations soar and their natural resources are overconsumed and otherwise depleted.

During the cold war, ideology mixed with political and economic considerations to prevent international cooperation in a wide variety of areas in which both factions had common interests. The Stockholm conference overcame political and economic division by highlighting those common interests and helped to set the stage for international cooperation that has continued to this day. A similarly divisive ideological milieu exists today between those who have accepted (at least generally) the norms and values associated with globalization, free enterprise, and democratic forms of governance and those who reject those norms and values. Because the eras of the cold war and the global war on terror are similar in their ideological and cultural divisiveness, a high visibility conference much like the Stockholm conference may be necessary to start a long-term process of new and continually evolving forms of international cooperation.

The United Nations and its operating agencies may continue to play important roles in addressing the problems of the fevered crescent, but the organization cannot form the center of the effort. It lacks both the organizational competence and internal political cohesiveness, and it is unlikely to strengthen itself substantially on either count. As the United Nations' inability to mobilize collective action against the 1994 genocide in Rwanda and the genocide in Sudan and the many years of corruption in its administration of the Oil for Food Program in Iraq all demonstrate, the world body is not as good at fixing certain types of problems as it is at identifying them. Identification is, however, an important first step, and the United States and other economically advanced nations of the world should begin working now with the nations of the Lagos-Cairo-Karachi-Jakarta arc to mobilize support in the General Assembly for a resolution calling for an international conference to draw attention to the economic underdevelopment and governance underdevelopment in emerging megacities.

A conference, too often, is just a meeting. To be successful, it must do what the 1972 Stockholm conference did and what some other conferences have done—change the mind-sets of the participants, including nongovernmental organizations as well as United Nations member states. A successful conference would impress upon the participants the severity of the security, economic, and environmental challenges that are emerging in the fast-growing megacities and depopulating rural areas of the fevered crescent and elsewhere. It would also demonstrate to the participants how absolutely critical it is that they reject the comfortable but misguided nostrum that these problems can be satisfactorily addressed by the current programs of the United Nations or the existing national approaches to foreign aid and development assistance. Finally, a successful conference would also generate public information and educational materials that would educate leaders and citizens about the benefits that will be derived from timely action.

A definitive conference agenda would undoubtedly generate more creative approaches than we offer here, but the following strategies ought to be given careful consideration. We list them here, in order, and detail them more fully below:

1. Increase reliance on regional organizations—with some cautions;

2. Reprioritize foreign aid;

3. Mobilize and encourage the coordinated targeting of private donations;

4. Develop international regimes to harness the positive effects of remittances on home countries, particularly in the fevered crescent;

5. Encourage the expansion of civil society organizations that contribute to urban infrastructure and governance;

6. Orient security assistance more toward security sector reform;

7. Revisit the concept of "security communities."

Increase Reliance on Regional Organizations—with Some Cautions

The most successful and enduring regional organizations have historically taken root in the soil of economically advanced parts of the world, specifically Western Europe and North America. The reasons are obvious: advanced states have both the wherewithal to invest in these organizations and the economic incentives for cooperation and mutual defense. The North Atlantic Treaty Organization is the apotheosis of an effective regional security organization. The European Union is new in comparison to NATO, but has demonstrated effectiveness in a number of political and economic areas. Longer lasting structures such as the League of Arab States, the Organization of Petroleum Exporting Countries, the Organization of American States, and the African Union (formerly the Organization of African Unity) have, unfortunately, proven themselves to be ineffective at organizing action beyond the expression of the membership's political position on the issues of the day. The League of Arab States, for example, has been widely criticized for building committee structures and holding meetings without ever translating this activity into tangible improvements in Arab cities and economies or, for that matter, even into effective military cooperation among its member states.[2]

Smaller regional organizations have evolved in recent years, largely for the coordination of economic policies and the harmonization of tariffs. Several of these organizations have evolved to the point where they are undertaking some of the steps that should be part of the overall approach to the challenges of the future. For example, the Economic Community of West African States (ECOWAS) has undertaken peacekeeping operations in Liberia and is considering a central bureau to coordinate regional approaches to terrorism and cross-border criminal activity. Compact regional organizations such as ECOWAS have advantages that large, more geographically dispersed organizations do not have.[3] Moreover, regional organizations have greater knowledge about local problems, cultures, and political constraints. They also often face fewer transportation and logistic hurdles in deploying peacekeeping forces in the region.

Further, many of the problems faced by less developed countries have transnational aspects and thus lend themselves to resolution by the nations that share the problem—unity of effort becomes easier when the parties have mutual interest in their resolution, as is more likely to be the case with smaller regional organizations. Too often, efforts to solve transnational problems have involved states that do not actually share the problem. In the various crises of Central Africa, for example, the West typically expresses fleeting interest. Interest by the wealthy states of North America, Europe, and East Asia will only become more sporadic, more transient when the focus shifts—as it ultimately must—to the domestic problems of states in the fevered crescent.

An obvious drawback to reliance upon regional organizations is that few are truly capable of marshaling and sustaining "nation-building" or extensive and intensive peacekeeping efforts. In much of the fevered crescent the reasons for the dearth of regional organization capability are relative poverty and rivalries among neighboring states.

The ineffectiveness of the League of Arab States is testimony to the latter factor. Arab states have been so busy undermining each other and propping up state-owned industries against competition from industries in other states that tangible cooperation among League members on important matters has proven impossible. For example, as late as 2004, the Arab leader of Libya was reported to have organized an attempted assassination of the de facto leader of Saudi Arabia and, at the time, the heir apparent to the Saudi throne, and in 2005 Syrian operatives were under investigation for assassinating a Lebanese leader.[4]

The League's membership is also probably too broad for effective action. In this sense the League resembles the United Nations, as these organizations have such diverse membership that it is difficult to formulate common approaches to problems that do not affect all members at least in roughly equal measure. The League and the UN also share a grossly uneven distribution of resources. Much of the collective wealth of the League members is concentrated in Persian Gulf states that, in terms of foreign aid and foreign policy, have been more interested in promoting cultural and religious causes than in working collectively to solve social, economic, and political problems in other states.

The African Union's membership is also too broad for effective action (some of its members are also members of the League of Arab States), but the AU is attempting to address this problem by building subcontinental response capabilities that could make it more nimble and effective. The AU is planning to establish standby military forces in each of five regions in Africa, and these units would be on call for AU and UN peacekeeping missions. In 2005 the AU took another step in the right direction by deploying units of cease-fire monitors to Darfur, Sudan. While it is true that the UN units were neither chartered nor equipped to actually suppress violence, it is also true that the AU's half measure was more than any other international organization has been willing to take in that desperate humanitarian crisis.

The solution must be for the United States and other developed countries to work together to maximize the effectiveness of investments in regional organizations—but not just by investing in their peacekeeping capabilities. In some instances this may even mean supporting the establishment of new regional organizations where the existing ones are too broad or too ineffective.

Nigeria, in this regard, is a worthwhile case study. The Nigerian military has been the backbone of ECOWAS peacekeeping efforts in Liberia and Sierra Leone. There has been controversy about the role that these peacekeepers played in both countries. For example, Human Rights Watch criticized the Economic Community of West African States Monitoring Group (ECOMOG) operations in Liberia in 1993 for causing excessive casualties among the civilian, noncombatant population and for attacking medical facilities that should have been treated as neutral sites.[5] Since 1993 there have been improvements in the precision and discipline of ECOMOG operations.[6] These improvements are certainly worthwhile, but it should be noted that improvements in ECOMOG's and Nigeria's ability to monitor cease-fires and engage militarily with armed factions in various West African states do not help Nigeria or the region address what may turn out to be the area's most important security challenge: the surge in urban population of Nigeria's main city, Lagos, and the domestic turbulence that has already begun to accompany the concentration of governance and economic resources in Lagos and its vicinity.

The peacekeeping capabilities of regional and subregional organizations can be assisted in several tangible ways. One is to make military equipment, especially transport vehicles and armored personnel carriers, available to them. Another is to assist in training and equipping the peacekeeping troops or to supporting the development of permanent training institutes in the region for peacekeepers.

The United States has operated two programs since the late 1990s to provide this training: the African Contingency Operations Training and Assistance (ACOTA) program and the African Crisis Response Initiative (ACRI). Approximately 6,000 African troops were trained under ACRI between 1997 and 2000. ACOTA replaced ACRI in 2001 and has since trained more than 9,000 troops.[7] A third and in some ways more important form of assistance to regional organizations is to oversee their peacekeeping operations. The oversight would be to ensure that they adhere to UN standards regarding respect for existing borders as well as for human rights and the protection of noncombatants. If there is a credible process for monitoring regional peacekeeping operations, confidence in the regional organization doing the peacekeeping will grow across the region and with it the organization's soft power to address other issues.

New regional organizations or subcomponents of existing organizations should also be fostered to address specific transnational problems, such as crime and terrorism. Models for these structures exist in Europe and North America where law enforcement agencies have long cooperated with each other and shared intelligence information. The war on terrorism has heightened cooperation among law enforcement and intelligence agencies worldwide, but there are gaps. Within the fevered crescent, more gaps are likely to develop as national governments strive to provide services and develop infrastructure in grossly overcrowded cities and remote rural provinces are more or less left to their own devices. Monitoring criminal, terrorist, and separatist group activity in these remote locations will likely be well beyond the capability of governments stressed by urban nightmares. Relying upon cooperative efforts with neighboring states to keep these areas under surveillance may be the only practical approach.

Related to the issue of criminal and terrorist activity in ungoverned rural areas is the question of weak or nonexistent border controls. The ability of armed groups to move freely among neighboring states in some regions (the

Afghan-Pakistan border, the eastern border of the Democratic Republic of Congo, the triangle where Paraguay, Argentina, and Brazil meet, Colombia's borders with Venezuela, Ecuador, and Brazil) reduces what little incentive there is for national governments to invest scarce resources in enforcing laws and asserting government control in some remote regions. The Afghan-Pakistan border is an extreme example and one to which there simply may be no practical solution because the terrain is so rugged and has so very little intrinsic economic or strategic value. But in some areas cooperative ventures in which border control is a shared bilateral function, even a function of a regional organization, could offer a less expensive, practical approach to the problem.

Cooperative ventures in keeping surveillance over remote areas and improving border controls may, for all their practical appeal, be resisted by states that are concerned about national sovereignty or about their neighbor's ulterior motives. Oversight of these functions by a credible third party such as the United States or a special UN commission or monitoring body might make these options more palatable and perhaps more effective as well.

Reprioritize Foreign Aid

Regional organizations should be given high priority in government foreign aid programs. Aid should also be prioritized in terms of the types of aid provided, and the focus should be broadened to enable the orchestration of the efforts of government and nongovernment donors toward common goals in the states of the fevered crescent.

Many nations, including the United States, routinely earmark foreign aid. That is to say, states use aid for foreign policy purposes, and these purposes do not always align with an objective assessment of the geographic location where the "need" is greatest. Often, the earmarking results in resources that could otherwise be used on economic development or social services being expended upon the acquisition of military hardware.

Nongovernmental organizations, and private sector foundations, also earmark aid—in the sense that they maintain ongoing humanitarian operations in the same countries for extended periods, in some cases for several decades. For example, Catholic Relief Services has been operating in Sierra Leone and the Democratic Republic of Congo for more than four decades.[8] This is not to say that the humanitarian needs in these countries are not real or deserving of attention, but rather that more than four decades of humanitarian operations in a particular country bespeaks a form of earmarking. Because an interruption in humanitarian aid could set back improvements in living conditions that have been carefully built over time, Catholic Relief Services is, in an admirable way, earmarking funds to Sierra Leone and the DRC in order to make their sunk costs good. Nongovernmental organizations also do something akin to earmarking on a functional basis according to their charters. Thus groups such as Médecins Sans Frontières target spending on meeting the medical needs of populations distressed by conflict or disaster, and Greenpeace International focuses on protecting the environment and endangered species. In these cases the funds are, in effect, earmarked to particular functions by the donors who decide for whatever reason which organization to support.

Earmarking is not the only factor. Governments also vary considerably in how they distribute aid. In some countries much of the aid is delivered outside government channels, through nongovernmental organizations. Most also distribute aid bilaterally on a government-to-government basis and through multilateral organizations such as the European Union's humanitarian office or one of the United Nations' agencies. This adds to administrative overhead and makes coordination for maximal effect considerably more complex.

States also vary considerably in the extent to which they offer official development assistance (ODA)—the term of art for foreign aid that is not emergency relief. (Emergency relief in this context consists of such things as distributing food in famine-stricken areas or tending to the medical needs of earthquake victims. ODA consists of expenditures for long-term economic development, such as building public health facilities and roads.) For example, according to statistics compiled by the Organization of Economic Cooperation and Development (OECD), almost three-fourths of Italy's ODA is distributed through multilateral organizations such as the UN or the World Bank. Only one-fourth of Italian ODA is "invested" bilaterally, that is to say, given directly by Italy to another country. Many other states invest 50–60 percent of their ODA funds bilaterally. In 2000, the two biggest ODA investors in terms of absolute dollars spent were the United States and Japan. Both invested almost three-fourths bilaterally and only one-fourth multilaterally.[9]

A more effective way would be to orchestrate a global approach to foreign aid that targets greater levels of foreign aid at the burgeoning urban populations in fevered crescent cities and on the states that are attempting to govern them. This is not only considerably easier said than done; it is unrealistic to believe perfect coordination of effort will ever be achieved. Official foreign aid has traditionally reflected the national interests and domestic political pressures of the donating states and will continue to do so as long as the world is organized around states.

There can, however, be sharp improvements in the coordination of foreign aid and the division of effort among bilateral and multilateral institutions. Foreign aid is a contentious issue. Its advocates are correct in pointing out that development programs have improved living conditions in many locations, and its critics are correct in countering that aid too often encourages dependency and that trade and investment are more effective vehicles for promoting growth.

A number of recent studies suggest that it is perfectly reasonable to expect—and even demand—some form of conditionality after civil conflicts, in particular. Just as any sagacious investor expects to see some form of return, so too should those supporting what Emma Rothschild has elegantly termed the "ceremonies of reconstruction" in the wake of conflict.[10] Donors of aid should begin to consider aid as an investment in the collective future, not as a palliative for the side effects of war. From warfare in Bosnia-Herzegovina to civil wars in Central America and West Africa and South Asia, it should be a routine, necessary expectation that post-conflict aid, investment, and debt relief should be linked to adherence to the terms of the peace accords and genuine commitment to governmental reform. Admittedly, this approach bears the appearance of a type of gentleman's bribery—and it probably is. Taken to extreme, withholding or withdrawing aid might well lead to the further weakening of already feeble states. That is why security sector reform should be pursued, as discussed below, in parallel with aid to reconstruction.

Both sides of the foreign aid divide concede that results could be improved if donors were to orchestrate their actions more effectively. As a recent World Bank study noted, aid works best when donors work together for common long-term goals instead of competing for political advantage or, in the case of private humanitarian organizations, for fund-raising publicity.[11] The community of donor nations should start now to focus on ways of improving coordination of aid programs in the arc of burgeoning cities between Lagos and Jakarta. As James Boyce has rightfully argued, investing in sustaining societies and regions requires not only reconstruction of war-torn places but also the reconstruction of aid itself.[12]

Mobilize and Encourage the Coordinated Targeting of Private Donations

In addition to ODA, there is a considerable amount of aid—and, of course, investment—that is contributed by the private sector outside government channels. For example, citizens, corporations, and foundations in the United States and other countries routinely donate funds directly to nongovernmental organizations, such as the aforementioned Catholic Relief Services and Médecins Sans Frontières, for expenditure in underdeveloped and/or disaster-afflicted states in eastern Europe, Africa, Asia, and Central and South America. These donations are substantial.

Overall, the total value of all private donations is larger than the total value of all bilateral and multilateral official aid combined.[13] For the United States, the dollar value of foreign aid provided by U.S. citizens, corporations, and foundations through private sector channels was almost $16 billion in 2000.[14] In Islamic countries, private sector donations through religious foundations are also more substantial than government foreign aid. (The Islamic practice of *zakat* obviously contributes to this phenomenon.) However, there are many countries in which private donations are small relative to the size of the national economy and in comparison with official aid amounts. This suggests that there are untapped private sector resources that could be mobilized.

Some forms of private sector aid have been controversial, in particular nominally charitable Islamic foundations that have been implicated in terrorist funding. The controversy, however, affects only a small proportion of all private donations, and efforts to track and suppress terrorist funding networks are probably sufficient to prevent controversies of this sort from arising in the future.

Of course, private sector donations are by their very nature outside the ambit of governments and are invested wherever the individual donor decides. This obviously makes coordination and orchestration of effort very difficult, as donors simply may not agree with all of the coordinated priorities and policies that will be necessary to begin making serious progress on the urban and rural problems described in this book. Furthermore, it is likely that efforts to impose greater government controls would be counterproductive. Instead of eliciting increased donations, heavy-handed government action is likely to demobilize existing donors and deter potential ones.

The challenge then is to mobilize private donations and encourage (but not require) these increased donations to be directed toward high-priority projects in the fevered crescent. This is a challenge, not a dilemma. The solution is to educate the public and the various foundations, corporations, and nongovernmental organizations that receive the donations about where their donations could best be put to use. The UN conference recommended above would be an appropriate vehicle for initiating the process.

The Organization of Economic Cooperation and Development already has a Development Assistance Committee whose job it is to coordinate the aid strategies of the most economically advanced countries in the world. The DAC could assume responsibility for continuing the donor-education process and for establishing vehicles for donors to channel their donations. This could, for example, mean encouraging donors to dedicate the majority of their contributions to organizations and projects with proven track records in the emerging megacities that feeble states are struggling to govern.

Develop International Regimes to Harness the Positive Effects of Remittances on Home Countries, Particularly Fevered Crescent States

Remittances are funds that are remitted or transferred from individuals in one country to individuals in another country. Typically, they are sent by expatriate workers who went abroad looking for better jobs and who support their families back home by sending them money they earn. Internationally, the sheer volume of remittances sent by migrants from outside their home states has grown remarkably, outstripping official development assistance and soon to outstrip all global foreign direct investment.

In 1990, migrant remittances amounted to less than half of the value of ODA, but by 2004 the situation had reversed. ODA has increased only slightly since 1990, while remittances have increased dramatically, and as a result remittances are now twice as substantial in terms of dollar value.[15] In 2005, officially recorded remittances worldwide reached an astounding $232 billion—with emerging states receiving $167 billion, more than twice the level of development aid from all sources. States receiving the most in recorded remittances are India ($21.7 billion), China ($21.3 billion), Mexico ($18.1 billion), France ($12.7 billion), and the Philippines ($11.6 billion). Moreover, some states depended heavily on such remittances in their total overall gross domestic products: Tonga (31 percent), Moldova (27.1 percent), Lesotho (25.8 percent), Haiti (24.8 percent), and Bosnia-Herzegovina (22.5 percent). And despite the emphasis on remittances from developed countries, remittances sent from developing countries—so-called South-South flows—represented 45 percent of total remittances.[16] In the case of France, the flow is to a developed country.

Thus, for some regions, the volume of remittances is truly substantial.

From the perspective of the United States, the most important flow of remittances is south toward Mexico, Central America and the Caribbean,
and South America. It has been estimated that more than $30 billion in
remittances flowed from the United States south in 2002 and that in the
same year the total value of all official foreign aid to the region was less
than $15 billion.[17] According to the Inter-American Development Bank,
the value of remittances was slightly higher in 2004, and the average Latin
American immigrant sent home approximately $1,800 in remittances over
the year.[18] To put this $1,800 in perspective, it is about half the per capita
GDP in some Latin American states and 20 percent of the per capita GDP
in Mexico.

Remittances also form a major source of income to countries in Africa,
the Middle East, South Asia, and Southeast Asia—the very regions that
face the most dire security, economic, and environmental challenges. For
example, India's economy gained an estimated $11.5 billion in 2002 from
remittances and Egypt's $3.7 billion. The Egyptian total was larger than the
amount received in both foreign direct investment and foreign aid.[19]

Remittances are almost always made to family members still in the home
country and are spent on food, clothing, and other forms of consumption. As
such they do increase economic activity, but they do not contribute directly
to economic development. There are, however, mechanisms being established in Mexico and some South American countries to increase the impact of remittances on development and, much less directly, on governance.
For example, the Organization of American States has sponsored a Pan-
American Development Foundation to help émigrés use remittance money
to invest in economic and infrastructure development in Mexico and El Sal-
vador. There is also a Transnational Community Development Fund that
enables legal émigrés in the United States to donate funds for development
projects back home. The United States supports this program by allowing
the donations to be deductible for tax purposes, and under some conditions
the donations are matched by the U.S. government and/or the home country.[20] Programs such as these should be expanded.

Another step that could be taken to increase the positive impact of remittances on the home country is to establish better banking systems, so that
émigrés would be able to send money home through banks, which would
then have larger reserves and could lend more money to development projects.[21] This would introduce greater transparency and regulation into local financial institutions, itself a valuable contribution to governance, and it
might elicit greater investments from émigré communities.

Remittances are, of course, private transfers between individuals and families, but a concerted effort to improve the mechanisms for remittance transactions and to create mechanisms for remittances to be invested in economic development in the home country should increase the resources available to key fevered crescent states such as Nigeria, Egypt, and Pakistan.

Encourage the Expansion of Civil Society Organizations That Contribute to Urban Infrastructure and Governance

Civil society organizations include a wide range of entities—labor unions, professional and trade associations, values-oriented organizations (such as environmental and human rights advocacy groups), and nongovernmental organizations that provide humanitarian and other services. Civil society organizations, in the main, serve useful functions and can help overwhelmed municipal and national governments provide essential services. They can be useful sources of technical assistance and advice about infrastructure construction and maintenance and the reorganization of municipal agencies. They can also help educate urban populations on community self-help and neighborhood-level political organization.

To some extent this is happening already. The Muslim Brotherhood, for example, provides important medical and educational services in many poor, underserved Cairo neighborhoods and isolated villages outside the metropolis. In many of the communities in which it operates, the Brotherhood provides more services than the Egyptian government does. As constructive as those services are, the Muslim Brotherhood's ideology and political objectives (fundamentally advocating Islamic law as the basis for government and associating themselves with terrorist violence) have put it at odds with the Egyptian government.[22] The Brotherhood's control of student and professional associations further puts it in the position of being perceived by the government as its main opposition.[23] Its history of violence against the regime causes many in Egypt and elsewhere to be skeptical of its good intentions, and this skepticism undoubtedly limits its effectiveness as an agent of governance reform and economic development.

Another example is the *madrassahs*, or religious schools that have been set up in poor communities in Pakistan, Sudan, and elsewhere to provide education to children whom the government does not service. These *madrassahs* are funded largely by Saudi Arabian charities and have a bad reputation because of their association with puritanical and antiwestern forms of Islam. By some estimates there are more than 40,000 of these schools in Pakistan, and their popularity has been tied to the collapse of the governmental educational system.[24] To some extent, the story of the *madrassahs* in Pakistan is a microcosm of the problem that governments throughout the fevered crescent will be facing. The *madrassah* system for training religious scholars existed long before there was a Pakistan, but the recent expansion of the system is a reflection of more than the oil wealth of Saudi Arabia. It is a reflection of the inability of the Pakistani government to meet the demands of a growing and increasingly urbanized population. This is, of course, hardly unique to Pakistan. In many other states there is a disparity between the supply of government services and the public's demand for those services, and the disparities will only grow wider as urban populations surge.

One solution for filling this growing gap in the Pakistani educational system and elsewhere is for NGOs, the UN, and donor nations to work together to sponsor civil society organizations that will, in effect, compete with the *madrassahs* in filling the void created by weak, overburdened governments.

Because of existing political tensions, Egypt would not be a good place to launch an effort to expand the reach of civil society organizations. But the idea of developing more politically neutral counterparts to the Muslim Brotherhood in other states does carry strategic weight. The idea will be resisted in many areas, for some of the same reasons that the Egyptian government casts a wary eye on Muslim Brotherhood activities. As civil society organizations become effective, they cause a redistribution of political power, something that authoritarian and nondemocratic regimes resist. Indeed, according to the *2003 Arab Human Development Report*, Egypt is not the only government in the Arab world that has been restricting the space available to civil society organizations. According to that same report, Syria, Saudi Arabia, and until recently Iraq were also hostile environments for civil society organizations that were independent of the government.

The prospects for developing indigenous civil society organizations to assist municipal governments may be few, but they should be explored wherever feasible. At the international level, attention could be given to promoting greater emphasis on municipal governance and infrastructure among nongovernmental organizations based in the West.

Orient Security Assistance More toward Security Sector Reform

It is well known that economic growth and domestic stability depend in no small measure on the rule of law. Establishing confidence in the administrative competence and integrity of the governmental organs charged with executing the law is one of the signal challenges facing many countries in the less developed parts of the world. Indeed, many of the states in the fevered crescent are renowned for the incompetence, corruption, and arbitrariness of their police, immigration, customs, licensing, and taxing agencies as well their court systems. In some of these states, private militias and undisciplined regular military forces that intervene in domestic affairs further complicate matters. Until such time as these "security sector" organizations and systems are reformed and public confidence in them is established, maintaining progress on other fronts will be difficult.[25] For example, essential long-term foreign and domestic investment in infrastructure and commercial ventures will remain limited as long as investors lack confidence in the predictability and competence of regulatory authorities.

The unstable security conditions in postwar Iraq and in the territory of the Palestinian Authority suggest how difficult security sector reform may be under certain circumstances. In these and other locations, efforts to establish control over multiple security sector organizations (Hamas and other Palestinian factions, for example, in Gaza) amounts to what can be seen as a virtual civil war among domestic factions with sharply divergent political agendas. The situation in Iraq also demonstrates that security sector reform may be more important over the long term than elections or the erection of checks and balances between the legislative and executive branches of government and between central and regional authorities. No apparently democratic government can succeed without ability to provide security or without minimum levels of confidence that security sector agencies have ceased to be predatory.

The issue, of course, is how the international community can constructively promote and assist security sector reform inside states in the fevered crescent. One way is to reorient security assistance programs. The bulk of security assistance provided by the United States and other countries has tended to involve military hardware, specifically aircraft, ships, communications gear, and conventional weapons. Because security assistance is consensual—that is to say, the recipient's desires are and should be taken into account—it may not be possible for any one country to unilaterally reorient security assistance away from the hardware that the recipient state's military wants to obtain. Moreover, in some cases there may well be a need for traditional military hardware, for example, to suppress an internal uprising or to maintain the balance of power against a regional adversary.

That said, efforts should be made to shift security assistance away from traditional military hardware and toward the nonlethal weaponry, crowd control gear, communications equipment, public outreach capabilities, and continuity of government capabilities that modern city governments

require. These requirements are particularly acute in many of the emerging megacities of Africa and south-southeast Asia. It is, indeed, one of the
enduring lessons of peacekeeping operations in Iraq, Haiti, the Balkans,
and Afghanistan that the maintenance of law and order is a sine qua non for
nation-building. It is no less true for governance-building in overcrowded
and undergoverned cities.

Revisit the Concept of "Security Communities"

In April 2000, Admiral Dennis C. Blair, commander of U.S. forces in the Pacific, spoke of moving from the balance-of-power Realpolitik among major
states that fundamentally characterized much of nineteenth-century Europe
to an alternative approach of security communities, "in which states concentrate on shared interests in peaceful development and actively promote
diplomacy and negotiation to resolve disagreements."[26] Admiral Blair's remarks, notably, drew on the work of a European, Karl Deutsch, who wrote
about the importance of security communities for cold war Europe over
four decades ago.[27] As equally notable was the reality that Admiral Blair's
remarks fell on deaf ears.

Yet the idea of such communities, especially in the fevered crescent of
emerging megacities, has relevance today and in the future. Various scholars
examining how states and regions deal with mutual, overlapping interests
have begun, once again, to struggle with this issue. Scholarship has, for example, addressed the development of "epistemic communities"—in essence,
networks of knowledge-based experts who might help develop common
interests, frame issues for collective debate, propose specific policies, and
identify issues that require negotiation, compromise, and agreement.[28] Such
communal approaches, rather than focusing on a realism-based state-to-
state interaction, acknowledge changing patterns of information diffusion
and decision making, and rely on transnational relationships, state admin-
istrators, and international institutions. This is, after all, more or less the
pragmatic approach that has been taken in the war on terrorism where experts from various national law enforcement and intelligence agencies work
together on suppressing terrorist financing, interdicting the transportation
of terrorist weapons, and preempting terrorist operations through timely
arrests even though the states for which these agencies and experts work are
unable to agree on broad policy issues.

Yet perhaps another pragmatic approach involves the South African Development Community (SADC), an international organization principally
dedicated to coordinating economic policies among its member states. Rec-

ognizing the interdependencies between economic, domestic governance, and security issues, the organization established a Ministry of Foreign Affairs, Defence, and Security and committed to a regional Mutual Defense Pact.[29] Perhaps the slow, often unwilling commitment of international agencies (almost always from outside the region itself) has led to the recognition at least in South Africa that states and peoples must learn to help themselves and each other—because no one else truly will.

Conceptual frameworks must build on the recognition that security communities, while evolving, remain viable alternatives to current and future security dilemmas. Policy commitments to such communities should incorporate flexibility enough to allow for inevitable contradiction yet provide structure able to accommodate change and provide the potential for progress. As the security environment evolves and as relationships between states and regions grow and become increasingly linked in complex interdependence, so too will the understanding, application, and relevance of new confidence and partnership-building measures.

In Lieu of Closure

It must be obvious to any reader that the policy prescriptions and recommendations offered here are hardly silver bullets—sure-fire, single-shot solutions. The issues confronting strained governments and feeble states are much too complex for quick fixes or single solutions. They will instead require decades of concerted effort.

The good news is that much of this effort is already under way, albeit in a dispersed manner requiring considerably sharper focus. Indeed, many of our recommendations call for improvements in existing programs and more effective tapping of existing resource flows.

There is also a risk associated with these recommendations. It is what economists call "in-group preference." That is to say, in programs such as the ones recommended here, there is a distinct possibility that efforts to improve the national security of the United States by strengthening governance in other countries may have antidemocratic consequences. In making governments more capable, we may also strengthen the hold of incumbents upon the reins of government—permanently.

This is, as many foreign policy analysts have observed, exactly what has happened in Saudi Arabia where the United States and the West in general have supported the ruling regime because it maintained stability in a critical oil-producing region. The regime has been supported despite its evident corruption, human rights abuses, and even indications that it has lost the

Fig. 7.1. The Real Map of the World

support of much of the Saudi population. Indeed, it was not until Saudi citizens were found to have played major roles in the September 11, 2001, attacks on the United States that U.S. support for the Saudi regime began to be critically reexamined. The fact that the reexamination did not result in a dramatic reversal of American relations with the Saudi ruling family is obviously a reflection of the continuing importance of oil to the world economy and the short-term desire of the West for Saudi cooperation in the war on terrorism. The result, whether intended or not, has been preference for the in-group in Saudi Arabia.

It is likely appropriate to end this wide-ranging meditation on the trends and effects that will fundamentally change the global environment—and the fevered crescent in particular—with a certain note of ambiguity. Perhaps it might help to conclude this discussion with the same possibilities with which we began.

Let us consider the image we offered in our first chapter. Referring again to the NASA composite satellite image, we begin to assess the unique measure of "the spatial extent of urbanization." The earthlights map compelled us to think about some disturbing trends and effects that, if left unchecked, will likely come back to haunt us in the coming decades. These developments, broadly considered here, are the changing demographics of cities, particularly in what we called the Lagos-Cairo-Karachi-Jakarta arc and the increased possibility of failing regions within functioning but troubled states.

By now, of course, we hope our argument that we must pay greater attention to the literal rural and figurative urban shadows on the earthlights map has been convincing. And while there seems to be an emerging understanding that certain nontraditional security issues that have long plagued the so-called developing world have circled back to haunt us, the solutions and responses to crises are far from evident. This is not to say that traditional state-centric security problems are things of the past or that military force will have no role to play. But the boomerang effect of these nontraditional security issues could increasingly affect the policy decisions and options open to the developed states. Anarchy, governmental collapse, ethnic rivalry, cultural grievances, religious-ideological extremism, environmental degradation, natural resource depletion, competition for economic resources, drug trafficking, alliances between narco-traffickers and terrorists, the proliferation of inhumane weapons, cyber war, and the spread of infectious disease threaten us all. In a globalizing economy, no one can be completely isolated from their effects.

As our understanding of security concerns broadens and deepens, the traditional assumption that states and governments are the sole guarantors of security will be increasingly challenged. The map of the future will depend on how we cope with the broader human dilemma. Addressing this dilemma will require sustainable development and governance-improvement strategies and must take into account the numerous trends outlined here—most particularly dramatic population growth in cities of feeble states. In the Lagos-Cairo-Karachi-Jakarta arc over the next two decades, more and more people will be compelled by economic or environmental pressures to migrate to cities that lack the infrastructure to support rapid, concentrated population growth. As they migrate, their governments will increasingly be stressed by their demand for services such as education, law and order, sanitation, public health protection, clean water, and electricity. As their governments come up short in meeting that demand, violence, instability, pollution, and disease will be exported—perhaps "only" locally from the city to nearby communities and neighboring states, but very possibly also to the economically advanced states of North America and Europe. This includes, of course, the United States.

All of these difficult choices cannot—and must not—be left to political leaders alone. Politicians necessarily are driven by often more pressing, near term issues and will never be renowned for persistent attention to the challenges of the distant future. This is particularly true for the types of complex, long-term issues we have examined in this book. Indeed, a bottom up revolution in ideas to reshape the map of the future is absolutely necessary. Such effort requires the combined, concerted actions of powerful governments, international agencies, nongovernmental organizations, and corporations—and people. The right decisions must focus on the long view and not just the next crisis; to do this wisely requires strategic attention, strategic planning, and strategic investment. These are functions that do not fall comfortably into the lap of most institutions or individuals. That is why we have placed such a strong emphasis on education through an agenda-setting United Nations conference and other measures to inform the world of the changes that are en route.

It is possible, nonetheless, to end on a note of optimism. One last glance at the earthlights map should force any reasonable observer to ask why the United States is all "in the light." Surely such "success" is not just the product of splendid geographic isolation. Africa and Australia, after all, are isolated just as much from other regions. Yet Australia is a model of relative stability and economic progress, and Africa has been plagued by insecurity and poverty. This final question is worth some rumination.

While the United States is hardly the model example for every state or region of the future, it is worthwhile to suggest that a sense of common purpose, commitment, and even confidence helped push this nation forward and into the light. There are signs in Africa and in the global responses to events such as the South Asian tsunami of December 2004 and the South Asian earthquake of 2005 that senses of common purpose have begun to develop. Perhaps harnessing these senses in the ways discussed above will provide the best hope for addressing problems that the states of the fevered crescent—and through them, the rest of the world—will face in the future.

Notes

Chapter 2. Pockets of Darkness

1. United Nations, Millennium Project, Task Force on Improving the Lives of Slum Dwellers, *A Home in the City*, 2005, 11, <www.unmillenniumproject.org/documents/ Slumdwellers-complete.pdf>. Other UN reports suggest that the rural population of less developed regions will stay roughly the same. Department of Economic and Social Affairs, *World Urbanization Prospects 2003*, 24 March 2004, 4, <www.un.org/ esa/population/publications/wup2003/2003WUPHighlights.pdf>.

2. Percentages derived from data in *World Urbanization Prospects 2003*, 5.

3. Marc Sageman, *Understanding Terror Networks*, Foreign Policy Research Institute, 1 November 2004. Sageman based his conclusions on a review of biographical information available on 400 terrorists.

4. United Nations Commission on Human Rights, *Report of the United Nations High Commissioner for Human Rights on the Human Rights Situation in Colombia*, 24 February 2003, 14.

5. Larry Thompson, "La Violencia in Colombia," <www.interaction.org/newswire/ detail.php?id=683>, accessed 31 July 2002.

6. Michael Shifter and Vinay Jawahar, "State Building in Colombia: Getting Priorities Straight," *Journal of International Affairs* 58, no. 1 (Fall 2004): 143.

7. U.S. Department of State, *A Report to Congress on United States Policy towards Colombia and Other Related Issues*, 3 February 2003, <www.state.gov/p/wha/rls/ rpt/17140.htm>.

8. Richard L. Millett, *Colombia's Conflicts: The Spillover Effects of a Wider War*, Strategic Studies Institute, U.S. Army War College, October 2002, 14–27, <www. carlisle.army.mil/ssi/pdffiles/PUB14.pdf>.

9. There are numerous studies of the Rwandan genocide and its aftermath in the DRC. For a vivid reconstruction of the crime and anarchy in and around the refugee camps, see Philip Gourevitch, *We Wish to Inform You That Tomorrow We Will Be Killed with Our Families: Stories from Rwanda* (New York: Farrar, Straus and Giroux, 1998).

10. International Crisis Group, *Congo at War: A Briefing on the Internal and External Players in the Central African Conflict*, ICG Congo Report no. 2, 17 November 1998, 18–25.

11. James F. Miskel and Richard J. Norton, "The Intervention in the Democratic Republic of Congo," *Civil Wars* 6, no. 4 (Winter 2003): 2–5; Paul S. Orogum, "Crisis of Government, Ethnic Schisms, Civil War, and Regional Destabilization of the Democratic Republic of Congo," *World Affairs*, Summer 2002, 28–29.

12. "The UN Gets Tougher in Congo," *Economist*, 10 March 2005, 67; Marc Lacey,

"Militia Fighters Kill 9 UN Peacekeepers in Congo as Instability Continues," *New York Times*, 26 February 2005, A6.

13. These UN Security Council Resolutions are available at <www.un.org/Docs/scres>.

14. UN News Service, "Delegates at UN Forum Tell of Alleged Cannibalism in DR Congo," 21 May 2003, <www.reliefweb.int/w/rwb.nsf/6686f45896f15dbc852567ae00530132/0bae8cac7cab1db749256d2e0007b7f4?OpenDocumentl>.

15. Central Intelligence Agency, *World Factbook 2002*, <www.cia.gov/cia/publications/factbook/geos/cg.html#Geol>; Imtiyaz Delawala, "What Is Coltan? The Link between Your Cell Phone and Congo," ABC News.com, 21 January 2002; Helen Vesperini, "Congo's Coltan Rush," BBC News, World: Africa, 1 August 2001.

16. Roger Cohen, "Paraguay Provides a Haven for Smugglers," *Wall Street Journal*, 23 December 1998, 1.

17. Phillip K. Abbott, "Terrorist Threat in the Tri-Border Area: Myth or Reality?" *Military Review* 84, no. 5 (September/October 2004): 51–52. *Newsweek* reported that there had been warnings from U.S. intelligence agencies that Hizbullah was active in the region. Mark Hosenball and Michael Isikoff, "Fighting Terror by Attacking—South America?" *Newsweek*, 9 August 2004, 7.

18. U.S. State Department, *Patterns of Global Terrorism, 2000*, April 2001, <www.state.gov/s/ct/rls/pgtrpt/2000/index.cfm?docid=2437>.

19. U.S. State Department, *Patterns of Global Terrorism, 2003*, 78, <www.state.gov/documents/organization/31943.pdf>.

20. Rex Hudson, *Terrorist and Organized Crime Groups in the Tri-Border Area (TBA) of South America*, Federal Research Division, Library of Congress, July 2003, 1–2, <www.fas.org/irp/cia/product/frd0703.pdf>.

21. Ibid., 72.

22. Johan J. Ingles-le Nobel, "Terrorism: New Initiatives against Islamists," *Jane's Intelligence Review* 5, no. 10 (October 1998): 15.

23. U.S. State Department, *Patterns of Global Terrorism*, 2003, 72.

24. Carlotta Gall, "Afghanistan Leader Vows Return," *New York Times*, 13 November 2004, A2.

25. U.S. State Department, *International Narcotics Control Strategy Report, 1999*, March 2000, <www.state.gov/g/inl/rls/nrcrpt/1999/>.

26. Alain Labrousse, "The FARC's and the Taliban's Connection to Drugs," *Journal of Drug Issues*, Winter 2005, 171–72.

27. Steven Philip Cohen, "A Distant Region Takes Center Stage: Pulling Up the Roots of Terrorism in South Asia," *Brookings Review* 20, no. 3 (Summer 2002): 39; Kristel Halter, "The Unholy Alliance: Pakistan, the Taliban, and Osama bin Laden," *Washington Report on Middle East Affairs* 20, no. 9 (December 2001): 88–90; U.S. State Department, "Background Note: Afghanistan," April 2005, <www.state.gov/r/pa/ei/bgn/5380.htm>.

28. The United Nations IRIN network has a report that "does not necessarily re-

flect the views of the United Nations," stating that al-Qaeda was involved in the destruction. "Afghanistan: Heritage Conference Draws Up Priorities," <www.irinnews.org/report.asp?ReportID=28034>. Some media coverage indicated that al-Qaeda influence was decisive: for example, Jason Burke, "Path to Destruction," *Manchester Guardian*, 5 May 2002; Alan Coulson, "Inside al-Qaeda's Hard Drive," *Atlantic Monthly*, September 2004. Indeed, the fact that the statues were destroyed in the sixth year of the Taliban regime suggests that the destruction was something that would not have been done without outside influence.

29. U.S. State Department, *Patterns of Global Terrorism* 2000, <www.usemb.se/terror/rpt2000/report2000.pdf>.

30. "Africa Conflict: Congo-Rwanda Tensions Heating Up," *Global Information Network*, 29 December 2004.

31. Central Intelligence Agency, *World Factbook 2002*, 10.

32. Zalmay Khalilzad and Daniel Byman, "Afghanistan: The Consolidation of a Rogue State," *Washington Quarterly* 23, no. 1 (Winter 2000): 66.

33. Joe Klein, "Closework," *New Yorker*, 1 October 2001, 45.

34. See Douglas S. Way, "Targeting Terrorists: Can GIS Lead the Attack?" <www.geoplace.com/gw/2003/0310_gw/0310cvr.asp>.

Chapter 3. Cities of Hope, Cities of Fear

1. Based on the United Nations Population Division, 2001 revision, *World Population Report: Population Estimates and Projections*, <www.un.org/esa/population/unpop.htm>.

2. United Nations, Department of Economic and Social Affairs, World Urbanization Prospects, 1999, 93 ff., <www.un.org/esa/population/publications/wup1999/WUP99CH6.pdf>; World Urbanization Prospects, 2001 revision, <www.un.org/esa/population/publications/wup2001/WUP2001–pressrelease.pdf>.

3. United States Agency for International Development, *Making Cities Work*, August 2002, <www.makingcitieswork.org/urbanWorld/profiles>.

4. Central Intelligence Agency, *World Factbook 2005*.

5. Ellen Brennan-Galvin, "Crime and Violence in an Urbanizing World," *Journal of International Affairs* 56, no. 1 (Fall 2002): 124.

6. Arguably, a reverse quarantine existed in France among disaffected Muslim youth in the impoverished suburbs of Paris. Although guaranteed the rights of citizenship, the lack of opportunity—especially economic—led to the outbreak of sustained nights of violence and riots in the fall of 2005.

7. U.S. Department of Transportation, *Lagos Airport Security Improved, Secretary Slater Finds*, press release dated 22 December 1999, <www.dot.gov/affairs/1999/dot22199.htm>.

8. U.S. Department of State, *Deputy U.S. Trade Representative Addresses U.S.–Nigeria Trade Council (Nigeria "key" to U.S.–Africa trade partnership)*, 6 June 2000, <usembassy.state.gov/nigeria/wwwhcf02.html>.

9. U.S. Department of Commerce, Census Bureau, <www.census.gov/cgi-bin/ipc/idbrank.pl>.

10. United Nations, *World Population Prospects*, 2004 revision, <esa.un.org/unpp/p2kodata.asp>.

11. United Nations, Department of Economic and Social Affairs, *World Urbanization Prospects*, 1999, 93 ff., <www.un.org/esa/population/publications/wup1999/WUP99CH6.pdf>; *World Urbanization Prospects*, 2001 revision, <www.un.org/esa/population/publications/wup2001/WUP2001–pressrelease.pdf>.

12. We must acknowledge here the work and thought of one of the coauthors on an earlier version of this project. Richard J. Norton, whose essay "Feral Cities" appeared in the Autumn 2003 (97–106) issue of the *Naval War College Review*, built on the metaphor of a phenomenon that a number of alternative-minded security analysts and futurologists have suggested for the last several decades. See <www.nwc.navy.mil/press/Review/2003/Autumn/art6–a03.htm>. Perhaps the most arbitrary component of defining a feral city potential for significant security impact would include the selection of a million inhabitants as a distinguishing characteristic. An earlier approach to this issue focused on megacities, cities with more than 10 million inhabitants. However, subsequent research indicated that much smaller cities could also become feral, and so the population threshold was reduced. For more information on concepts of urbanization, see Stanley D. Brunn, Jack F. Williams, and Donald J. Zeigler, *Cities of the World: World Regional Urban Development* (Lanham, Md.: Rowman and Littlefield, 2003), 5–14.

13. Norman Myers, *The Gaia Atlas of Future Worlds: Challenges and Opportunities in an Age of Change* (New York: Anchor Books, 1990), 83.

14. As anecdotal support for why security forces most often follow policies of containment in rural zones, P. H. Liotta spoke privately and at length with a senior military officer in Rio de Janeiro who had operated inside the feral zones of that city. Ordered to lead a Marine helicopter raid into one of the most notorious favelas of the city, the officer related that he had little or no direction on how to conduct the raid other than to apprehend a specific list of individuals. When asked what the rules of engagement were for others not specifically targeted for arrest, he received vague advice. "What should I do," he asked, for example, "if a ten-year-old boy is holding a Kalashnikov in our face as we land?" He was told, "That decision will have to be yours." Fortunately, that decision never had to be made, but the officer did tell us that he had made up his mind before the raid that he was perfectly set on killing anyone, including a child, who stood in his way. And although the raid was conducted as planned—basically landing on a high hilltop of garbage and shanties and working down through individual homes and seizing specific targets as they presented themselves—there was also a level of frustration. Within a week, all the apprehended suspects were back, free, inside the feral city. That same week, intelligence intercepts tracked what appeared to be the sale by favela overlords of Stinger antiaircraft missiles to drug traffickers, possibly FARC guerrillas of Colombia. "The answer to this

problem," the officer told us, "is not a military one. After all, we are not cops. And even the cops can't solve this."

15. "China Criticized for Dragging Feet on Outbreak," *News in Science*, 7 April 2003, 1.

16. "Marburg Haemorrhagic Fever in Angola—Update," World Health Organization, 23 March 2005.

17. Joanna Mateus, "WHO Resumes Combating Virus in Angola," Associated Press, 10 April 2005; "WHO Operating Again in Angola on Marburg Virus Mission," *Medical News Today*, 11 April 2005.

18. The issue of pollution stemming from coastal cities is well documented. For example, see chapter 2 of United Nations Environmental Program, *Global Environmental Outlook 2000* (London: Earthscan, 2001).

19. The profits involved in such enterprises can be staggering. For example, the profits from smuggled cigarettes in 1997 were estimated to be as high as $16 billion a year. Among the identified major smuggling centers were Naples, Hong Kong, and Bogotá. Raymond Bonner and Christopher Drew, "Cigarette Makers Are Seen as Aiding Rise in Smuggling," *New York Times*, 26 August 1997, C1.

20. As Norton notes in fn. 17 of his "Feral Cities" essay, "While the rescue of Army Private First Class Jessica Lynch during the 2003 Iraq War demonstrates that success in such operations is not impossible, U.S. experiences with hostages in Iran, Lebanon, and Somalia would suggest failure is a more likely outcome." Furthermore, critical information leading to Lynch's rescue stemmed from Iraqi human intelligence; in feral cites, many occupants may well be suspicious of those alien to their environment.

21. Compiled from a variety of sources, most notably "Taming Mexico City," *News Hour with Jim Lehrer*, transcript, 12 January 1999, <www.pbs.org/newshour/bb/latin_american/jan-jun99/mexico>. Originally noted in Norton.

22. Peter Goodwin, "City of Hope, City of Fear: Johannesburg," *National Geographic*, April 2004, 64–65.

23. Compiled from a variety of sources, including BBC, UN, and CIA reports.

24. Ellen Liberman, "The Code Breaker," *Rhode Island Monthly*, June 2004, 43.

25. Discover Gauteng, *Gauteng Factfile: Vital Statistics* (Johannesburg, South Africa: Gauteng Tourism Authority, 2004), 6.

26. Equally, the security prospects for Johannesburg and Mexico City have largely improved since the mid-1990s, and some of the more dire predictions should be measured against cyclical periods of crime and violence, reflective of numerous urban centers.

27. Remarks by Sir Edward Clay to a meeting of the British Business Association of Kenya, "Address of High Commissioner Clay to the British Business Association of Kenya," *Daily Nation*, 14 July 2004, <www.nationmedia.com/dailynation/magcontent entry.asp?category_id=39&newsid=11534>. Notably, most editorials that appeared in journals and newspapers following High Commissioner Clay's address were highly

critical and even indignant that a "foreigner" would dare to criticize the government of Mwai Kibaki, despite its obvious problems. Subsequent editorials in the *Nation*, however, were more supportive of Clay's position, one even noting that "Britain, in any case, is not just any country with which Kenya has diplomatic relations. It has huge property here. How it acquired that property, of course, is a matter which political activists will always raise." Indeed, since the *Nation* is under the publishing ownership of His Royal Highness Aga Khan IV, a major development benefactor in Kenya through the Aga Khan Development Network (AKDN), Kenya is reluctant to confront him or his holdings in any direct way.

28. "Where Graft Is Merely Rampant," *Economist*, 18 December 2004, 65.

29. "Feet of Clay: More Bad News for Honest Kenyans," *Economist*, 12 February 2005, 48.

30. Clay, *Nation*.

31. For a review of Transparency International's "Corruption Surveys and Indices," see <www.transparency.org/surveys/index.html#cpi> (6 April 2004).

32. Philip Caputo, *Ghosts of Tsavo: Stalking the Mystery Lions of East Africa* (Washington, D.C.: Adventure Press, National Geographic Society, 2002), 33–34.

33. Myers, *Gaia Atlas*, 82.

34. *Matatu* stems from the Swahili word for "three," rather than "taxi." The exact origins and meanings are unclear, but according to the author's driver, the original cost for such vehicle transport was three Kenyan shillings. Others claim that the meaning rises from the number of crowded passengers.

35. In an unrelated incident, one in which a domestic employee was suspected of stealing, the subsequent interrogation of the employee was itself a bit horrific. The official noted that, on the few occasions when he had visited police stations, he always heard either screams or the sounds of beatings taking place, and almost always saw physical evidence of abuse on those he saw in cells. Notably, after the suspect theft incident at the official's residence, his *askari* related that the police immediately threatened the domestic with torture unless she confessed immediately to all she knew. Quaking with fear, she complied.

36. Robert D. Kaplan, "The Coming Anarchy: How Scarcity, Crime, Overpopulation, Tribalism, and Disease Are Rapidly Destroying the Social Fabric of Our Planet," *Atlantic Monthly*, February 1994.

37. Caputo, *Ghosts of Tsavo*, 54, 151.

38. Clay, *Nation*.

39. We stress that Kenya's population growth rate has declined significantly since independence. Whereas in the early 1970s the growth rate was at 4 percent or higher, the estimate was revised down to between 3.5 and 3.8 percent in 1989, and the Central Intelligence Agency growth rate estimate for 2005 was 2.65 percent. Kauli Mwenbe, "Kenya's Challenge: Population Growth and the Economy," *Multinational Monitor* 10, no. 5 (May 1989); *Pub Med*: A Service of the National Library of Medicine and the National Institute of Health, *Africa Population News*, no. 61 (July–December

1991): 11–12; Central Intelligence Agency, *World Factbook 2005*, "Kenya," <www.cia.gov/cia/publications/factbook/geos/ke.html>.

40. Jared Diamond, *Collapse: How Societies Choose to Fail or Succeed* (New York: Viking, 2005), 311–12.

41. Central Intelligence Agency, *World Factbook 2004*, data as of 10 February 2005, <www.cia.gov/cia/publications/factbook/geos/pk.html>.

42. Kurt Jacobsen, Sayeed Hasan Khan, and Alba Alexander, "Building a Foundation: Poverty, Development, and Housing in Pakistan," *Harvard International Review* 23, no. 4 (Winter 2002): 20–24.

43. "Karachi: It Is a Dirty Place but Who Cares?" *EuropaWorld*, 12 July 2001, <www.europaworld.org/issue60/karachi71201.htm>.

44. UN Office for the Coordination of Humanitarian Affairs, IRIN-News, "Pakistan: Karachi Water Shortage," 16 January 2002, <www.irinnews.org/report.asp?ReportID=19178&SelectRegion=Central_Asia&SelectCountry=PAKISTAN>.

45. Zarar Khan, "Pakistan's Doctors Protest at Killing of 13 Colleagues This Year," *British Medical Journal* (international ed.), 6 April 2002, 805.

46. The highest number of genocidal killings since World War II took place in Cambodia during the 1970s; the second worst genocide was in Bangladesh in 1971 (then known as East Pakistan). Notably, Rwanda's population is 10 times smaller than Bangladesh, making the Rwandan genocide all the more horrific.

47. Diamond, *Collapse*, 314.

48. Michael Renner, "New Threats to Human Security Study Documents Causes of New World Disorder," WorldWatch Institute, 26 October 1996, <www.worldwatch.org/press/ news/ 1996/10/24/> (13 April 2005). For further detail, see Michael Renner, *Fighting for Survival: Environmental Decline, Social Conflict, and the New Age of Insecurity* (New York: Norton, 1996).

49. Diamond, *Collapse*, 325–26. The first section of quotation is a secondary quote by Diamond from Belgian economists Catherine André and Jean-Philippe Platteau. Further thoughts on rural community involvement in human security issues can be found in Jean-Marie Baland and Jean-Philippe Platteau, *Halting Degradation of Natural Resources: Is There a Role for Rural Communities?* Foreword by Mancur Olson, a publication of the Food and Agricultural Organization of the United Nations (New York: Oxford University Press, 1996), as analysis in Catherine André and Jean-Philippe Platteau's paper "Land Relations under Unbearable Stress: Rwanda Caught in the Malthusian Trap," *Journal of Economic Behavior and Organization* 34 (1998): 1–47.

50. Diamond, *Collapse*, 324–28.

51. Secondary reference by Diamond, *Collapse*, 328. Further background is available through Gérard Prunier, *The Rwandan Crisis: A History of Genocide* (New York: Columbia University Press, 1995).

52. World Bank, "Mexico at a Glance," 16 September 2004, <www.worldbank.org/data/countrydata/aag/mex_aag.pdf>.

53. World Bank, "South Africa at a Glance," 15 September 2004, <www.worldbank. org/data/countrydata/aag/zaf_aag.pdf>.

54. Central Intelligence Agency, *The World Factbook 2004*, <www.cia.gov/cia/ publications/factbook/rankorder/2004rank.html>.

55. World Bank, "Pakistan at a Glance" 27 January 2005, <www.worldbank.org/ cgi-bin/sendoff.cgi?page=/data/countrydata/aag/pak_aag.pdf>.

56. World Bank, "Egypt at a Glance," 20 September 2004, <www.worldbank.org/ cgi-bin/sendoff.cgi?page=/data/countrydata/aag/egy_aag.pdf>.

57. World Bank, "Bangladesh at a Glance," 17 September 2004, <www.worldbank. org/cgi-bin/sendoff.cgi?page=/data/countrydata/aag/bgd_aag.pdf>.

58. Ellen Brennan-Galvin, "Crime and Violence in an Urbanizing World," *Journal of International Affairs,* Fall 2002, 56, 123.

59. See <www.genocideinterventionfund.org/GIF_index.php> (7 April 2005). (Note: Now listed as "The Genocide Intervention Network," <www.genocideintervention.net/ GIF_index.php>.)

60. Princeton N. Lyman, "*The Terrorist Threat in Africa*," Testimony before the House of Representatives in Southern Africa Hearing on Fighting "Terrorism in Africa," 1 April 2004, <wwwc.house.gov/international_relations/108/Lym040104.htm> (7 April 2005).

61. See <www.state.gov/s/ct/rls/other/14987.htm> (7 April 2005).

62. Lyman testimony.

Chapter 4. Rethinking Security

1. In recent debates, including those in *Security Dialogue,* a proliferation of descriptors have been added to the basic term *security.* Each of these descriptors lends a perhaps slightly different connotation as well. To speak of cultural security, economic security, environmental security, ethnic security, gender security, geographic security, human security, military security, physical security, political security, psychological security, or societal security suggests specific (and probably necessary) recognitions. It also unduly privileges these recognitions with discrete identities that depend on, and often cannot exist without, other identities. Admittedly, some of these security distinctions establish important linkages to policy and security decisions. Two recent examples include Sean Kay, "Globalization, Power, and Security," *Security Dialogue* 35, no. 1 (2004): 9–25, and Gunhild Hoogensen and Svein Vigeland Rottem, "Gender Identity and the Subject of Security," *Security Dialogue* 35, no. 2 (2004): 155–71.

2. James C. Scott, *The Moral Economy of the Peasant: Rebellion and Subsistence in Southeast Asia* (New Haven: Yale University Press, 1976), 1.

3. Hugh Courtney, Jane Kirkland, and Patrick Viguerie, "Strategy under Uncertainty," *Harvard Business Review,* 1 November 1997, 66–79.

4. For an extended discussion of this phenomenon, see P. H. Liotta, "Chaos as Strategy," *Parameters,* Summer 2002, 47–56, <www. carlisle.army.mil/usawc/ Parameters/02summer/liotta.htm>.

5. Fen Montaigne, "Water Pressure," *National Geographic*, September 2002, 2–33.

6. Richard Manning, "The Oil We Eat: Following the Food Chain Back to Iraq," *Harper's*, February 2004, 43–45.

7. Emma Rothschild, "What Is Security? The Quest for World Order," *Daedulus: The Journal of the American Academy of Arts and Sciences* 124, no. 3 (1995): 53–98.

8. UNDP, *UN Human Development Report* (New York: Oxford University Press, 1994), 3, 22–23.

9. UN Commission on Human Security, "Protecting and Empowering People," <www.humansecurity-chs.org/finalreport/outline.html>.

10. H. Richard Niebuhr, *The Responsible Self: An Essay in Christian Moral Philosophy* (San Francisco: Harper and Row, 1978), 52, 61–65, 88.

11. For examples of the "capabilities" approach, see the draft report of the DAC Informal Network on Poverty Reduction, <www.etcint.org/PDF/DAC%20vol%20I. pdf> (25 October 2004), as well as the United Nations Environment Programme report, *Exploring the Links: Human Well-Being, Poverty, and Ecosystem Services* (Winnipeg, Manitoba: International Institute for Sustainable Development, 2004) and Amartya Sen, *The Standard of Living* (Cambridge: Cambridge University Press, 1987).

12. The concept that social justice, participatory freedom, and economic development are social and security stabilizers is taken from Ian Barbour, *Ethics in an Age of Technology: The Gifford Lectures*, vol. 2, *1990–1991* (San Francisco: Harper, 1993), 26. Barbour's criteria form an appraisal of intervention and security as they apply to the relevant aspects of human values and social life.

13. Kyle Grayson: "Securitization and the Boomerang Debate: A Rejoinder to Liotta and Smith-Windsor," *Security Dialogue* 34, no. 3 (1 September 2003): 337–43; "A Challenge to Power over Knowledge in Traditional Security Studies," *Security Dialogue* 35, no. 3 (1 September 2004): 357.

14. Reinhold Niebuhr, *Moral Man and Immoral Society: A Study in Ethics and Politics* (New York: Scribner, 1932), 22.

15. John Rawls, *A Theory of Justice* (Cambridge: Belknap Press of Harvard University Press, 1973), 453, 454.

16. Timothy Garton Ash, "Europe's Endangered Liberal Order," *Foreign Affairs* 77, no. 2 (March/April 1998): 64–65.

17. Robert Kagan, "America's Crisis of Legitimacy," *Foreign Affairs* 83, no. 2 (March/April 2004): 75.

18. Jack Goldstone, "Population and Security: How Demographic Change Can Lead to Violent Conflict," *Journal of International Affairs* 56, no. 1 (2002): 3–21.

19. See, for example, Grayson, "Securitization and the Boomerang Debate."

20. Norman Myers, "The Environmental Dimension to Security Issues," *Environmentalist* 6, no. 4 (1986): 251–57.

21. Michael O'Hanlon and P. W. Singer, "The Humanitarian Transformation: Expanding Global Intervention Capacity," *Survival* 46, no. 1 (Spring 2004): 77–99.

22. See Thomas P. M. Barnett, "The Pentagon's New Map: It Explains Why We're

Going to War and Why We'll Keep Going to War," *Esquire*, March 2003, 174–81, and *The Pentagon's New Map: War and Peace in the Twenty-first Century* (New York: Putnam, 2004).

23. Astri Suhrke, "[Human Security:] A Stalled Initiative," *Security Dialogue* 35, no. 3 (2004): 365.

24. J. Peter Burgess, "Commentary," *Security Dialogue* 35, no. 3 (2004): 278.

Chapter 5. Governance and Democracy

1. Central Intelligence Agency, *World Factbook 2005*, <www.cia.gov/cia/publications /factbook/geos/ni.html>.

2. Congressional Quarterly, *The Middle East*, 9th ed. (Washington, D.C.: CQ Press, 1999), 224.

3. National Intelligence Council, Central Intelligence Agency, *Global Trends 2015: A Dialogue about the Future with Nongovernment Experts*, December 2000, <www. cia.gov/nic/PDF_GIF_global/growth_in_megacities.gif>.

4. United Nations Department of Economic and Social Affairs, *World Urbaniza- tion Prospects: The 2003 Revision Population Database*, <esa.un.org/unup/>.

5. Los Angeles Almanac, *Historical Resident Population: City and County of Los Angeles, 1850–2000*, <www.losangelesalmanac.com/topics/Population/po02.htm>.

6. Pini Jason, "Nigeria Still One Nation, One People," *New African*, April 2005.

7. Organization for Economic Cooperation and Development, *Final Develop- ment Assistance (ODA) Data for 2003 and Simulation of ODA Prospects for 2006*, 14 February 2005, <www.oecd.org/dataoecd/19/52/34352584.pdf>. According to an NGO, Trocaire, ODA declined by 10 percent in real terms between 1992 and 2002. Trocaire, "ODA: Global Levels," <www.trocaire.org/policyandadvocacy/oda/ globalodalevels.htm>. Trocaire is the official overseas development agency of the Irish Catholic Church.

8. United Nations, *UN Millennium Development Goals*, <www.un.org/millenniumgoals />.

9. United Nations, *Millennium Development Goals: Progress Report 2004*, 3, <www.un.org/millenniumgoals/mdg2004chart.pdf>.

10. Samuel P. Huntington, *Political Order in Changing Societies* (New Haven: Yale University Press, 1968).

11. Robert D. Kaplan, *A Sense of the Tragic: Developmental Dangers in the Twenty- first Century*, <www.nwc.navy.mil>, as well as reports of the State Failure Task Force referenced later herein.

12. Bill Clinton, *A National Security Strategy of Engagement and Enlargement* (Washington, D.C.: Government Printing Office, February 1995), i.

13. Ibid., 22–23. During an extended conversation by one of the authors with Anthony Lake, former national security adviser to President Clinton and chief architect of the first three editions of Clinton's *National Security Strategy of En- largement and Engagement*, Lake denied that Francis Fukuyama's provocative essay

"The End of History?" which originally appeared in *The National Interest,* Summer 1989, had much to do with the Clinton strategies. But a cursory examination of the strategies suggests otherwise. According to Fukuyama, for "modern" societies only some form of parliamentary democracies and open economic market systems are the viable choices for identity and governance—and indeed those principles are rooted in the very foundations of both the Clinton and second Bush administration strategies.

14. Bill Clinton, *National Security Strategy for a New Century,* May 1997, 19–20; October 1998, 33–34; and December 1999, 25 (Washington, D.C.: Government Printing Office).

15. George W. Bush, *The National Security Strategy of the United States,* September 2002, i and 4, <www.whitehouse.gov/nsc/nss.pdf>. The March 2006 "updated" Bush strategy is available at <www.whitehouse.gov/nsc/nss/2006/nss.pdf>.

16. John Ikenberry, "Why Export Democracy?" *Wilson Quarterly,* Spring 1999, 56–65.

17. Daniel C. Esty, Jack A. Goldstone, Ted Robert Gurr, et al., *State Failure Task Force Report: Phase II Findings, Environmental Change, and Security Project Report,* Summer 1999.

18. Ibid., 49.

19. John Steinbruner, *Principles of Global Security* (Washington, D.C.: Brookings Institution Press, 2000), 151.

20. Jeffrey D. Sachs, "The Strategic Significance of Global Inequality," *Washington Quarterly* 20, no. 3 (Summer 2001, 187–98).

21. Fareed Zakaria, "Islam, Democracy, and Constitutional Liberalism," *Political Science Quarterly,* Spring 2004, 1–2.

22. Shireen Hunter, *The Future of Islam and the West: Clash of Civilizations or Peaceful Coexistence?* (Washington, D.C.: Praeger, 1998), 35–36; Iliya Harik, "Democratic Thought in the Arab World," in Charles Butterworth and I. William Zartman, eds., *Between the State and Islam* (New York: Cambridge University Press, 2001), 150; Monte Palmer, *The Politics of the Middle East* (Itasca, Ill.: Peacock, 2002), 25–26; John L. Esposito, *What Everyone Needs to Know about Islam* (New York: Oxford University Press, 2002), 152, 159–60; Vartan Gregorian, *Islam: A Mosaic, Not a Monolith* (Washington, D.C.: Brookings Institution Press, 2003), 94–95.

23. Ray Takeyh, "Islamism in Algeria: A Struggle between Hope and Agony," *Middle East Policy* 10, no. 2 (Summer 2003): 65.

24. Gregorian, *Islam,* 79.

25. Pierre Azzi, "Harsh Rule: Recognizing the Taliban," *Harvard International Review* 21, no. 2 (Spring 1999): 13–14; Barnett R. Rubin, "Afghanistan under the Taliban," *Current History* 98 (Spring 1999): 80.

26. Khabir Ahmad, "UN Condemns Taliban's Continued Human Rights Abuse in Afghanistan," *Lancet,* 28 August 1999, 752.

27. Béchir Chourou, "Security Partnership and Democratization," in Hans Günter

Brauch, Antonio Marquina, and Abdelwahab Biad, eds., *Euro-Mediterranean Partnership for the Twenty-first Century* (London: Macmillan, 2000), 187.

28. John Lukacs, *Democracy and Populism* (New Haven: Yale University Press, 2005), quoted as "When Democracy Went Wrong," *Harper's*, April 2005, 17–18.

29. Ibid., 18.

Chapter 6. Foreign Policy Implications

1. Michael Scardaville, "The Cost of Securing the Homeland," *The World and I*, August 2003, 54.

2. Jack A. Goldstone, Ted Robert Gurr, et al., *State Failure Task Force Report, Phase III Findings*, 30 September 2000, v, <www.cidcm.umd.edu/iscru/stfail/SFTF%20Phase%Report%20Final.pdf>.

3. Hans-Herik Holm, "A Disaggregated World Order in the Making: Policy towards Failed States as an Example," *International Politics* 38 (September 2001): 358; Gerald Halman and Steven Ratner, "Saving Failed States," *Foreign Policy* 89 (Winter 1992): 3; Robert H. Dorff, "Democratization, Failed States, and Peace Operations: The Challenge of Ungovernability," *American Diplomacy* 1, no. 2 (1996); I. William Zartman, "Posing the Problem of State Collapse," in Zartman, ed., *Collapsed States: The Disintegration and Restoration of Legitimate Authority* (Boulder: Lynne Rienner, 1995); Nancy J. Walker and Larry Hanauer, "EUCOM and Sub-Saharan Africa," *Joint Forces Quarterly*, Spring 1997, 103–4; Daniel Thurer, "The 'Failed State' and International Law," *International Review of the Red Cross*, December 1999, 731–32.

4. Julio A. Cirino, Silvana L. Elizondo, and Geoffrey Wawro, "Latin America's Lawless Areas and Failed States: An Analysis of the 'New Threats,'" in Paul D. Taylor, ed., *Latin American Security Challenges: A Collaborative Inquiry from North and South*, Newport Paper (Newport: Naval War College Press, 2004), 8, 21, 22, 29, 31, and 32.

5. Susan E. Rice, *The New National Security Strategy: Focus on Failed States*, Brookings Institutions Policy Brief, no. 116, February 2003.

6. Robert I. Rotberg, "Failed States in a World of Terror," *Foreign Affairs* 81, no. 4 (July/August 2002): 127–28. In another 2002 article, Rotberg places greater emphasis on the humanitarian consequences of state failure than on the terrorist threat. Robert I. Rotberg, "The New Nature of Nation-State Failure," *Washington Quarterly* 25, no. 3 (Summer 2002).

7. Princeton N. Lyman and J. Stephen Morrison, "The Terrorist Threat in Africa," *Foreign Affairs* 83, no. 1 (January/February 2004): 75; Jeffrey Record, "Collapsed Countries, Casualty Dread, and the New American Way of War," *Parameters* 32, no. 2 (Summer 2002): 4–5; Herman J. Cohen, "The United States and Africa: Non-vital Interests Also Require Attention," *American Diplomacy* 8, no. 3 (2003).

8. Lyman and Morrison, "The Terrorist Threat in Africa," 80.

9. James A. Phillips, "Somalia and al-Qaeda: Implications for the War on Terror," *Heritage Foundation: Backgrounder #1526*, 5 April 2002, <www.heritage.org/Research/NationalSecurity/BG1526.cfm#pgfId=1014348>.

10. U.S. State Department, *Patterns of Global Terrorism 2003*, April 2004, 7, <www.state.gov/s/ct/rls/pgtrpt/2003/>.

11. U.S. Commission on National Security in the Twenty-first Century, *New World Coming: American Security in the Twenty-first Century*, 15 September 1999, 4–6.

12. U.S. Commission on National Security in the Twenty-first Century, *Seeking a National Strategy: A Concept for Preserving Security and Promoting Freedom*, 15 April 2000, 13.

13. Jusuf Wanandi, "Indonesia: A Failed State?" *Washington Quarterly* 25, no. 3 (Summer 2002).

14. *State Failure Task Force Report*, 135.

15. Reported in Center for Defense Information, Russia Weekly #255. "Russia Using the United States as a Buffer in Central Asia," *Nezavisimaya Gazeta*, 30 April 2003.

16. Thomas P. M. Barnett, "The Pentagon's New Map: It Explains Why We're Going to War and Why We'll Keep Going to War," *Esquire*, March 2003.

17. Samuel Huntington, "The Clash of Civilizations?" *Foreign Affairs* 72, no. 3 (Summer 1993): 22–49.

18. Thomas P. M. Barnett, *The Pentagon's New Map: War and Peace in the Twenty-first Century* (New York: Putnam, 2004), 88, 93, and 188–89.

19. Cirino, Elizondo, and Wawro, "Latin America's Lawless Areas and Failed States," 23–25.

20. Robert S. Chase, Emily B. Hill, and Paul Kennedy, "Pivotal States and U.S. Strategy," *Foreign Affairs* 75, no. 1 (January/February 1996): 33–51.

Chapter 7. A New Covenant

1. The text of the Declaration may be accessed at <www.unep.org/Documents/Default.asp?DocumentID=97&ArticleID=1503>.

2. United Nations Development Programme, *Arab Human Development Report 2003* (New York: UN Publications, 2003).

3. Among the recent examinations of the potential contributions of regional organizations are Michael Hirsh, "Calling All Regio-Cops," *Foreign Affairs* 79, no. 6 (November/December 2000): 2–8; Paul Omach, "The African Crisis Response Initiative: Domestic Politics and Convergence of National Interests," *African Affairs*, January 2000; Eric G. Berman and Katie E. Sams, "The Limits of Regional Peacekeeping in Africa," *Peacekeeping and International Relations*, July/August 1999; and James F. Miskel and Richard J. Norton, "Humanitarian Early Warning Systems," *Global Governance* 4, no. 3 (July–September 1998).

4. Michael Isikoff, "Libya: The Strongman Is Still Making Trouble," *Newsweek*, 1 November 2004; United Nations, *Report of the International Independent Investigation Commission Established Pursuant to Security Council Resolution 1595 (2005)*, 52–53, <www.un.org/news/dh/docs/mehlisreport/>.

5. Human Rights Watch, *Liberia: Waging War to Keep the Peace*, June 1993, <www.hrw.org/reports/1993/liberia/#8>, accessed 28 October 2004.

6. Adekeye Adebajo, *Building Peace in West Africa: Liberia, Sierra Leone, and Guinea-Bissau* (Boulder: Lynne Rienner, 2002).

7. The number of trained troops is drawn from a U.S. State Department report dated 13 October 2004. The report is available at <usinfo.state.gov/af/Archive/2004/Oct/14–232582.html>.

8. Catholic Relief Services, "Giving Hope to a World of Need: Our Work," undated, <www.catholicrelief.org/our_work/where_we_work/overseas/Africa/sierra_leone/index.cfm> and <www.catholicrelief.org/our_work/where_we_work/overseas/Africa/democratic_republic_of_congo/index.cfm>, accessed 29 October 2004.

9. United States Agency for International Development, *Foreign Aid in the National Interest* (Washington, D.C., 2002), 134.

10. Emma Rothschild, "What Is Security? The Quest for World Order," *Daedalus: The Journal of the American Academy of Arts and Sciences* 124, no. 3 (June 1995): 53–98.

11. International Bank for Reconstruction and Development, World Bank, *Assessing Aid: What Works, What Doesn't, and Why* (New York: Oxford University Press, 1998).

12. James K. Boyce, *Investing in Peace: Aid and Conditionality after Civil Wars*, Adelphi Paper 51 (Oxford: Oxford University Press, 2002).

13. World Bank, Millennium Development Goals, chapter 8, "Build a Global Partnership for Development," target 12–15, September 2004, < www.developmentgoals.org/Partnership.htm>, accessed 9 November 2004.

14. United States Agency for International Development, *Foreign Aid in the National Interest*, 134.

15. Devesh Kapur and John McHale, "Migration's New Payoff," *Foreign Policy*, November/December 2003, 48–58.

16. "Migration Can Deliver Welfare Gains," adapted from the World Bank 2006 *Global Economic Prospects* Report, <web.worldbank.org/WBSITE/EXTERNAL/TOPICS/EXT POVERTY/0,,contentMDK:20724214~pagePK:148956~piPK:216618~theSitePK:336992,00.html>.

17. Inter-American Dialogue, Task Force on Remittances, *All in the Family: Latin America's Most Important International Financial Flow*, January 2004, 4.

18. Inter-American Development Bank, *Remittances from the U.S. to Latin America 2004*, <www.iadb.org/exr/remittances/ranking.cfm>.

19. Internal Organization for Migration, *Migration Policy Issues no. 2: Facts and Figures on International Migration*, 2, <www.iom.int/DOCUMENTS/PUBLICATION/EN/MPI_series_No_2_eng.PDF>.

20. Michele Wucker, "Remittances: The Perpetual Migration Machine," *World Policy Journal* 21, no. 1 (Summer 2004): 40.

21. International Bank for Reconstruction and Development, World Bank, "Appendix A: Enhancing the Developmental Effects of Workers' Remittances to Developing Countries," *Global Development Finance 2004: Harnessing Cyclical Gains for Development* (Washington, D.C., 2004): 172.

22. John Walsh, "Egypt's Muslim Brotherhood: Understanding Centrist Islam," *Harvard International Review* 24, no. 4 (Winter 2003): 32.

23. Ninette S. Fahmy, "The Performance of the Muslim Brotherhood in the Egyptian Syndicate: An Alternate Formula for Reform?" *Middle East Journal*, Autumn 1998, 555–56.

24. P. W. Singer, "Pakistan's Madrassahs: Ensuring a System of Education Not Jihad," *Brookings Analysis Paper #14*, November 2001, 1–2, <www.brookings.edu/dybdocroot/views/papers/singer/20020103.htm>.

25. One of the most cogent primers on this subject is Jane Channa, *Security Sector Reform: Issues, Challenges, and Prospect*, Adelphi Paper 344 (Oxford: Oxford University Press, 2002).

26. Dennis C. Blair, "Security Communities Are the Way Ahead for Asia," *International Herald Tribune*, 21 April 2000, <www.iht./IHT/TODAY/FRI/ED/edblair.html>. Other useful works that address security communities include Ernst B. Haas, *The Uniting of Europe* (Stanford: Stanford University Press, 1958), and more recently Emmanuel Adler and Michael Barnett, eds., *Security Communities* (Cambridge: Cambridge University Press, 1998). Notably, although Deutsch stressed the importance of values, learning, and socialization for security communities, he drew the conclusion that European integration had effectively stopped by 1958.

27. Karl Deutsch, *Political Community and the North Atlantic Area* (Princeton: Princeton University Press, 1957).

28. See, in particular, Peter M. Haas's introduction on "Epistemic Communities and International Policy Coordination," in a special issue devoted to epistemic communities, *International Organization* 46 (Winter 1992): 1–36.

29. See, in particular, Naison Ngoma, "SADC's Mutual Defence Pact: A Final Move to a Security Community?" *Round Table* 93, no. 375 (July 2004): 411–23, <www.sadcreview.com/sadc/frsadc.htm>.

Index

James F. Miskel is a consultant and a former professor of national security affairs and associate dean of academics at the U.S. Naval War College. He served on the National Security Council under two presidential administrations. Recent work includes *Disaster Response and Homeland Security: What Works, What Doesn't.*

P. H. Liotta is professor of humanities at Salve Regina University and executive director of the Pell Center for International Relations and Public Policy in Newport, Rhode Island. Recent work includes *The Uncertain Certainty: Human Security, Environmental Change, and the Future Euro-Mediterranean; The Exile's Return: Selected Poems* (published in the Macedonian language), and the coauthored *Gaia's Revenge: Climate Change and Humanity's Loss.*